WHOPPERS

WHOP

HISTORY'S MOST OUTRA

ZEST BOOKS

PPERS

GEOUS LIES AND LIARS

BY CHRISTINE SEIFERT

Connect with Zest!

- zestbooks.net/blog
- zestbooks.net/contests
- twitter.com/zestbooks
- facebook.com/BooksWithATwist

35 Stillman Street, Suite 121, San Francisco, CA 94107 / www.zestbooks.net

Manufactured in the U.S.A.
DOC 10 9 8 7 6 5 4 3 2 1
4500542185

CONTENTS

PREFACE

When I was a kid, my mom told my brother and me that we'd get a black dot on our foreheads if we told a lie. My brother fell for it immediately, but I was more suspicious. I told a lie and then ran to the mirror to check for evidence. No black dot. I learned two things that day: First, Mom had no idea when I was lying. Second, Mom was a liar too. And so a fascination with liars began. Why do people lie? What do they lie about? Who believes these lies? Why?

We've all been lied to, probably every day. Some of the time we can spot these lies and the liars who tell them, even without black dots. Everybody in my junior high knew that nerdy little Jackson Hoff didn't really play bass for the Red Hot Chili Peppers, even though he swore it was true. And everybody knew that our government teacher, Mr. Richards, didn't really throw a chair at a student, even though he bragged about having done so. And everybody knew that our junior high wasn't really haunted, but we all claimed it was, just to freak each other out. So lies aren't a big deal because only the most naive and gullible people actually believe them, right?

Wrong.

History is full of liars. Not just little-white-lie liars, but big-honkin', whopper-telling liars who convinced a lot of people that even the most improbable, outrageous, nonsensical stories are true. And the worst part is this: We'll believe them. Sometimes liars even believe themselves.

Some of the lies in this book are funny. Some of them are really gross (so be careful if you have a weak stomach). Some of these lies hurt a lot of people. Some of them cost people money. Sometimes liars don't even realize when they are lying because they want so badly to believe. Other times the lies aren't lies at all but wacky stories that people believed to be true nonetheless.

Lying is generally wrong. That's not up for discussion, but you have to admit that liars and lies are often interesting. This book will tell you about some of history's biggest and most interesting hucksters, tricksters, scam artists, pretenders, and just plain old pathological liars.

Get ready, because some of these stories will blow your socks off. And that's no lie.

— CHRISTINE SEIFERT

SECTION 1:
TALL-TALE TELLERS

What's the biggest tall tale you've ever told? No matter what it was, I'm willing to bet the people in this chapter told stories that were crazier than anything you are likely to imagine.

Before you get started, take this quiz to find out if your tall tales are as wild as the tales told by history's biggest liars.

HOW BIG OF A TALL-TALE TELLER ARE YOU?

Answer the following questions with "yes" or "no." No lying!

1. Have you claimed your parents, siblings, or friends were rabbits? Like, actual rabbits?
2. Have you told people you think eating babies is perfectly okay?
3. Have you created a mermaid out of a monkey head and a fish fin, and then charged your friends to see it?
4. Have you claimed to have discovered an island full of human-eating natives?
5. Have you written stories about Christopher Columbus and claimed they were all totally, completely true?
6. Have you claimed a dead body was cursed?
7. Have you built a giant horse, filled it with soldiers, and attacked your enemies within the walls of their own city?
8. Have you claimed your pet horse can do algebra?
9. Have you made up a story about the president's toilet?
10. Did you invent a disease to sell something people didn't even know they needed?
11. Have you told your friend — just before he bites into his double bacon cheeseburger — that the burger is made out of poop?

If you answered **no** to all of these questions, congratulate yourself. You are a very honest human being. You should be proud of yourself. What kind of person pretends a cheeseburger is made out of poop? (Oh, just wait. You'll see.)

If you answered **yes** to any of these questions, you are a tall-tale teller. And you have much in common with history's biggest liars. You might want to see somebody about your lying. •

CHAPTER 1:
HARD-TO-BELIEVE-ANYONE-BELIEVED STORIES

MARY TOFT

DATE: 1726

THE LIE: That she gave birth to rabbits

REASON: For money and fame

Mary Toft had a plan to get rich. At twenty-five, she was married to Joshua, a poor cloth-worker, but Mary wanted more from life than just being a housewife. So she cooked up a scheme to "get so good a living that I should never want as long as I lived." Mary decided to tell her neighbors — and any doctors who would listen — that she'd given birth to a monster.

In the eighteenth century, people loved looking at monsters. They would pay big money to see weird stuff, like a giant, a bearded lady, a two-headed woman, a two-bodied man, a boy with a live bear growing from his back, mermaids. You get the picture. Not surprisingly, most of these people were great big frauds, but that didn't stop them from making a whole lot of money. Mary decided she was going to get on this gravy train.

Her first monster baby was actually a cat — a dead cat — with its limbs cut off and its guts removed. She slipped an eel backbone (a convenient left-over from Sunday dinner) through its intestines. Ta-da. Instant monster baby.

She pretended to give birth to the cat creature and then called her neighbors to examine the monster. (Can you imagine getting that call?) The disgusted neighbors sent for John Howard, a surgeon who thought the whole thing was pretty suspicious. He said he wouldn't believe Mary unless he saw the cat's head.

Unfortunately, Mary had lost the head.

Fortunately, John Howard wasn't so smart. He was fooled by Mary, who improvised. She had no cat head, but she did have a rabbit head handy. Now she really had something to write home about. A cat with an eel backbone and a rabbit head! This was bound to make her the talk of the town, if not the whole of England.

John could hardly believe his eyes. It was good news for him because the doctor who discovered the woman who gave birth to cat-eel-rabbit babies would most certainly become rich and famous too. He stuck around while

THE ELEPHANT MAN

Mary Toft wasn't the only person in history believed to have turned her baby into an animal by maternal impression.

In 1862, Joseph Merrick was born with severe facial deformities. He was nicknamed the Elephant Man. Why? Because when his mother was pregnant with him, she was accidentally knocked over by an elephant at a fair. Joseph believed that was the reason for his elephant-like head.

Mary pretended to give birth to almost twenty more rabbit creatures over the course of a few weeks.

Word got around that Mary Toft was a rabbit mother. Even King George I heard about it. He sent Nathaniel St. André, the official Surgeon and Anatomist to the Royal Household, to investigate. Nathaniel might have been skeptical at first, but he soon believed Mary was affected by some supernatural force. The king was intrigued by this news.

All these doctors and scientists — all men, by the way — had a reasonable explanation for Mary's bunny babies. That explanation was something called "maternal impression." At the time, a lot of smart people believed that if something scared a pregnant woman or occupied her mind, it would affect her unborn baby. Mary claimed to have been startled by a rabbit in a field. After that, she craved rabbit meat for months. John and Nathaniel decided that was explanation enough for her rabbit babies.

Of course we now know there's no such thing as maternal impression. Thank goodness. I might have been born as a big bowl of popcorn. And you might have been a hot fudge sundae.

Mary's scheme might have continued if not for King George, who sent ever more skeptical doctors to investigate. One of those doctors was Cyriacus Ahlers, a German, who came up with the brilliant idea of investigating rabbit poop. You read that right. He looked at poop.

He figured out that if Mary's rabbit babies grew inside her womb, they wouldn't have straw or hay or corn in their poop. Rabbits in the womb would have nice, creamy milk poop. Mary's rabbits had corn poop. That's how Cyriacus knew then that Mary was faking.

By this time, however, lots of people wanted to believe that Mary was a rabbit mommy. It was probably pretty exciting. Imagine if something like that happened today. We'd post it all over Instagram. Mary would be on every TV talk show.

If John and Nathaniel had their doubts, they kept them quiet. They had a lot to lose. After all, they were respected doctors who had publicly proclaimed Mary's rabbit babies to be the real deal. Nathaniel himself claimed to have seen with his own eyes a rabbit "leaping in her Belly, for a space of eighteen Hours, before it dy'd." He even wrote a book about Mary. It's called *A Short Narrative of an Extraordinary Delivery of Rabbets*.

Mary might have made a lot of money and lived the rest of her life in the lap of luxury if not for a London porter. Her doctors brought her to London to observe her, which made it hard to pretend to give birth to dead rabbits. It's not like she could call room service for some rabbits.

Well, except that's sort of what she did. She had her sister-in-law ask the porter to bring her a small rabbit. He ratted on Mary. (Rabbited on her?)

Mary was forced to admit the whole thing was a hoax done for the money. (She blamed her mother-in-law for coming up with the scheme.)

John and Nathaniel were royally teed off, mostly because they looked like morons. Nathaniel wrote an article for the *Daily Journal* two days after Mary confessed and said, "I am now thoroughly convinc'd it is a most abominable Fraud." Now you say so, buddy.

People all over England mocked the doctors. These men claimed to be expert medical scientists, yet they'd been fooled by an illiterate woman. And they couldn't figure it out until the poop guy arrived and the porter tattled on her.

Lucky for Mary that everyone was so embarrassed. A legal case against her was dropped, though she was pronounced a "Notorius and Vile Cheat."

KING GEORGE I

King George I, who was fascinated by Mary Toft, was a weird guy who loved oddities of all sorts. In 1725, German villagers discovered a hairy wild child emerging from the forest. He was naked, walked on all fours, and ate grass and leaves. Villagers captured him and put him in jail because they didn't know what else to do with him. Then King George I came to town. He was fascinated by the wild child. He named him Peter and took him back to court to be his pet. King George taught Peter the Wild Boy to do tricks like a trained dog. When the king tired of Peter, he sent him to live on a farm.

Mary didn't make any money from her hoax, but she got more than her fifteen minutes of fame. Here we are, almost 300 years later, and we still talk about Mary Toft as the woman who gave birth to rabbits.

That's quite a way to be remembered. •

JONATHAN SWIFT

DATE: 1729

THE LIE: That eating humans was an excellent idea

REASON: To show people what a ridiculous idea eating babies was. (You gotta wonder about people who needed to be convinced.)

Before Taylor Swift, there was **Jonathan Swift**. (About the only thing they have in common is the same wavy hair. Taylor's is probably real, though. Jonathan wore one of those powdered wigs popular with eighteenth-century men.)

You might know Jonathan Swift from a novel he wrote in 1726 called *Gulliver's Travels*, about a guy named Lemuel Gulliver who meets a bunch of tiny people in a place called Lilliput. (You might have seen the movie in 2010 where Jack Black plays Gulliver. There's also a 1939 Paramount Pictures version of the movie.)

Well, after Jonathan wrote about Gulliver and tiny people the size of Crayola skinny markers, he wrote an essay that got a lot of people upset. You see, Jonathan was understandably angry about the way England was treating people in Ireland.

Jonathan cared a lot about Ireland because that's where he was born in 1667. When he was only a year old, his nanny kidnapped him and took him to England. Fortunately, he was reunited later with his mother in Ireland. After he graduated from Trinity College in Dublin, he decided it was time to return to England. He got a job as a secretary to an important politician, Sir William Temple. In addition, Jonathan became a writer of poems, stories, odes, essays, political pamphlets, and satires. And he also became a priest in the Church of Ireland. He was a pretty busy guy.

One of the things that bothered Jonathan most was the attitude people in England had about poor people in Ireland. Ireland was essentially a colony of England, which meant that England controlled almost every aspect of life in Ireland, including the government. On top of that, most of the land in Ireland was owned by English landlords who collected a lot of money from poor Irish workers who could barely feed their families. England was basically the school bully who demanded Ireland's lunch money. Jonathan thought that England was being a real jerk, and he wanted everyone to know that. So he wrote an essay about it.

"A Modest Proposal for Preventing the Children of poor People in Ireland from being a Burden to their Parents or Country; and for making them beneficial to the Publick" is a short essay with a very long title. In the essay, Jonathan suggests that poor Irish people should sell their children to English people, who could eat them.

Let me repeat that in case you think you read it wrong: Jonathan suggests that English people should eat babies! Jonathan's essay even details delicious ways to cook and eat them. He writes, "A young healthy child well nursed is at a year old a most delicious, nourishing, and wholesome food, whether stewed, roasted, baked, or boiled; and I make no doubt that it will equally serve in a fricassee or a ragout."

Some readers thought Jonathan was serious, but he wasn't. He wasn't exactly lying, but he wasn't saying what he meant either. He was doing something called satire. Satirists use exaggeration and irony — which is when you say the opposite of what you mean — to expose something that's ridiculous or wrong. In this case, Jonathan wanted readers to know that *of course* eating babies is a bad idea — just like a lot of other ideas the English came up with were bad ideas that didn't help the poor Irish. What would help the Irish would be to give them food. It was really as simple as that.

Readers who didn't understand satire thought Jonathan was being serious. (We have to hope they didn't actually eat any babies in a fricassee or a ragout.) When they discovered he wasn't serious, they wanted to know why

MÉNIÈRE'S DISEASE

Jonathan Swift had Ménière's disease, which is a disease of the inner ear. Jonathan suffered from dizziness, depression, headaches, and hearing problems because of it, but he was never officially diagnosed with it because the doctor who identified the condition, and for whom it is named, did not do so until the mid-1800s.

Another famous person suffered from the same disease. Did you know that the painter Vincent van Gogh had it too? Maybe that explains why he cut off his ear!

JONATHAN SWIFT ON FARTING

Jonathan Swift was very serious about poverty in Ireland, but that wasn't the only topic he wrote about. He also wrote an essay called "The Benefit of Farting Explained." Jonathan believed women would feel better if they just farted more. He identified "five or six different species of farts." Those included the "sonorous and full-toned, or rousing fart," "double fart," "soft fizzing fart," "wet fart," and "sullen wind-bound fart."

This is a man who took farting very seriously. He describes each one in detail and discusses his own experience letting each of these types of farts rip.

I think it's safe to say that Jonathan Swift was a fan of lady farters.

he didn't say what he meant in the first place. But Jonathan knew that saying what you don't mean or believe is a good way to get people's attention. And if you do it well, you can make a really important point.

In the case of "A Modest Proposal," Jonathan made many readers realize that they had to stop suggesting ridiculous ideas about how to fix Ireland when the real problem was poverty. And you don't have to be an Einstein to figure out how to help poor people.

Jonathan wanted people to laugh but then look at themselves and wonder what they could be doing differently. Jonathan was a bit of a downer, though, because he said satire "is a sort of glass [mirror], wherein beholders do generally discover everybody's face but their own." He means that satire helps us see other people's mistakes but not always our own.

"A Modest Proposal" might be hundreds of years old, but people still read and talk about it. And many people still use that phrase — "a modest proposal" — to refer to an ironic plan that we would never really do. It signals that people are saying the opposite of what they mean. In essence, satire is a kind of socially acceptable lie that can make people think.

So put down your fork: Nobody is going to eat any babies. •

P.T. BARNUM

DATE: Beginning in the 1840s

THE LIE: Where to begin? How about that he had a mermaid skeleton? That's just one of his lies

REASON: Money and fame

You've certainly been to a circus before, but I guarantee that you have never seen anything like **Phineas Taylor (P.T.) Barnum**'s displays. Before he had a circus, he had a museum that was a collection of weird things, like taxidermy, art, an aquarium, live opera performances, a wax museum of figures, and newfangled technology. All these curiosities were displayed in Manhattan at Barnum's American Museum. It opened in December of 1841, and people went nuts for the over 800,000 exhibits that took up five stories. Where else, they reasoned, could you pay a relatively small amount to see machines that talked? Or Siamese twins?

P.T. didn't feel bad at all about tricking his customers; in fact, that was his specialty. One time he claimed to have a model of Niagara Falls inside his museum. People couldn't wait to pay money to see it. Turned out P.T. did have a Niagara Falls model, but it was only eighteen inches tall and emitted just a tiny stream of water.

Always looking for ways to make a dime, P.T. liked to capitalize on people's stupidity. He once put up a sign in his museum that said "This Way to the Egress." People wanted to see what egress was so they followed the sign right out the door. And then P.T. charged them again to come back into the museum! (Do you get the joke? Egress means exit. P.T. was lucky that his customers had small vocabularies.)

You've probably heard of one of P.T.'s most famous exhibits: General Tom Thumb, Man in Miniature. Tom was actually Charles Sherwood Stratton, and he was two feet tall and four years old. P.T. taught little Charles how to sing and dance, and told audiences he was eleven years old and from England. Tom Thumb was so popular that even Queen Victoria of England wanted to see this tiny boy. When Charles got older, P.T. contracted a dwarf girl named Lavinia Warren to be Mrs. Tom Thumb. Thousands attended

MORE LIKE PINOCCHIO T. BARNUM

their wedding reception. In his autobiography, P.T. swears that Tom and Lavinia married for love. As a result of Tom and Lavinia, P.T. made pails of money. (It helped that P.T. only paid Charles three dollars a week to perform. Eventually, Charles got a raise and made twenty-five dollars a week.)

One of P.T.'s other famous exhibits was the Feejee Mermaid. He claimed to have on display a real-life mermaid skeleton that he acquired from Dr. J. Griffin. Dr. J. argued that all animals have a sea counterpart. So just as there's a lion, there's a sea lion. Apparently, Dr. J. assumed that because a land maid exists, so too exists a sea maid (a mermaid). Dr. J. wrote letters to newspapers about his discoveries. Readers of the *New York Times* were ecstatic when the mermaid skeleton showed up at P.T.'s museum. The *New York Sun* called it the "deucedest looking thing imaginable." You know that it must have been creepy and amazing to earn the adjective *deucedest*.

Eventually, people learned that the mermaid was a fake. It was just an ape head sewn to a fish body. Turns out that such monstrosities were common in Japan. Japanese fishermen made "mermaids" all the time — they even considered it an art. P.T., never one to miss an opportunity, decided that he could make money on some of this weird mermaid art. He hired Dr. J., whose real name was Levi Lyman, to pretend to be a naturalist studying mermaid remains. P.T. made sure that Dr. J./Levi sent plenty of letters to the papers about his supposed work. And if that didn't catch readers' attention, there were the sexy mermaid pictures that accompanied the articles. By the time Dr. J./Levi arrived in New York with his mermaid, people were ready to pay money to see a gorgeous sea-lady. Imagine how disappointed they were when they got nothing but an ape-fish.

P.T. was never short on creative schemes. One of his first exhibits was an old woman named Joice Heth. P.T. claimed she was 161 years old and formerly George Washington's nanny. People from all over the country were eager to see what our first president's nanny looked like. The answer: old. In reality, she was an eighty-year-old former slave whom P.T. bought for about a thousand dollars. When people got tired of looking at an old lady, P.T. told everyone she was an automaton — a kind of robot. And do you know what happened? People paid to see her again for the opportunity to catch a glimpse of her supposed robotic parts.

In his autobiography, P.T. writes proudly of all the other tricks he devised for his audiences. For example, he had a little girl in his employ who would sit on stage and fake being in a state of deep sleep. While she fake-slept on stage, P.T. called a member of the audience to the stage and claimed he could put that audience member "in the same state" as the little girl or give the audience member fifty dollars. The audience member would accept the challenge and agree to let P.T. hypnotize him with his magical abilities. Of

FAMOUS NAMES

Tom Thumb isn't just the name of the little person in P.T.'s traveling show. It's also the name of a convenience store chain in Alabama and Florida. There are more than 100 of them in the southern part of the United States.

FOUR ELEPHANT FACTS
(BECAUSE WHAT'S A CIRCUS WITHOUT ELEPHANTS?)

1. Elephants have walked the earth for more than fifty-five million years.
2. Adult elephants weigh between 10,000 and 12,000 pounds. That's like five or six SUVs!
3. Elephants live for about forty-five years. That's probably how old your parents are.
4. Elephants can remember individual people and animals for years, even after they've been separated.

course P.T. had no such abilities. The wide-awake audience member would exclaim, "Aha! Give me my fifty dollars!" Only then would the little girl speak up and claim she was not asleep at all. She was faking the whole time. P.T. would then tell the audience member that he indeed was in the "same state" as the little girl: wide awake.

Brilliant, right? P.T. sure thought so. He wrote in his autobiography, "I quite killed" with that trick. And the trick had the added benefit of making mesmerism — a form of hypnotism that was very popular at the time — look like a joke or a dumb party trick.

P.T.'s kooky humor delighted people at a time when entertainment was supposed to be refined and educational. P.T. — even though he loved the opera and other high culture — provided an accessible kind of entertainment that anyone could enjoy.

You know enough about P.T. now that you won't be surprised when I tell you that he started his career as a showman and money-maker early in his life. Before he was thirteen, he sold lotto tickets and rum to soldiers. He perfected his art of promotion and showmanship for years. When he was sixty, he debuted his circus at the Great Roman Hippodrome (which you might know better as Madison Square Garden). He made almost $500,000 in the first year. In 1872, he proclaimed P.T. Barnum's Grand Traveling Museum, Menagerie, Caravan, and Circus to be "The Greatest Show on Earth."

P.T. did not have a self-esteem problem. That's for sure. •

CHAPTER 2:
EXOTIC
FABRICATIONS

THE LIAR:

GEORGE PSALMANAZAR

DATE: 1704

THE LIE: That he was a native from an exotic island called Formosa

REASON: For the heck of it

George Psalmanazar (an alias) had pale white skin, blond hair, and a Dutch accent, yet he still convinced a lot of smart people that he was from the Far East and spoke Japanese. People in Europe didn't know much about faraway lands, so they believed him, a fact that probably surprised even George himself at first.

George was born sometime between 1679 and 1684, probably in France. When he was a young man, he joined the Dutch army and, for reasons nobody knows, pretended to be a person from Japan who spoke Latin. It's unclear whether his army buddies believed him or if they just said, "Yeah, sure, George, you're Japanese. We totally believe you." He told them that the Jesuits tricked him into leaving Japan, and since the Dutch were suspicious of Jesuits in general, they liked hearing George talk smack about them.

While in the Netherlands, George met Chaplain Alexander Innes, who was a pretty smart guy. Chaplain Alexander devised a test to prove whether or not George spoke Japanese. Chaplain Alexander asked George to translate a passage of Cicero (written in Latin) into Japanese. George, clever liar that he was, just translated it into gibberish. After all, Chaplain Alexander didn't know Japanese. But Chaplain Alexander was the cleverer of the pair: He asked George to translate it a second time. And guess what happened? Yup, George couldn't translate Cicero into the same gibberish. (There's a lesson in here: Don't translate into a gibberish language even *you* can't remember.)

You might assume that the jig was up for George, but something fascinating happened. Chaplain Alexander decided not to tell anyone that George was a big fraud. Chaplain Alexander kept his trap shut because he wanted to baptize George. He thought that would look good for

Christianity if he could produce a real-life exotic convert from a faraway land. It was Chaplain Alexander who told George to tell people he was from Formosa, a more exotic hometown than Japan. At the time, nobody knew anything about the island of Formosa. You probably know it by its name today: Taiwan.

And so George went to London to tell everyone there all about his adventures as a primitive island dweller. Fortunately for George, he had quite an imagination, and he convinced almost everyone that he was the real deal, a Formosa transplant experiencing civilization for the first time. He told gullible Londoners all kinds of things about Formosa that he just made up. Here are some of his strange lies.

- Formosa villages floated, like giant houseboats.
- Formosa natives only ate raw meat. (To prove his point, he only ate heavily spiced raw meat while in London.)
- Formosa natives slept sitting up. (And so George slept in a chair.)
- Formosa natives spoke in tongues. (Nobody questioned him when he suddenly started spouting gibberish.)
- Formosa natives worshipped the moon. (Maybe he just needed an excuse to stand outside and howl.)
- Formosans sacrificed 20,000 boys per year to the gods. (These were apparently some demanding gods.)
- Formosan priests ate body parts from the unlucky boys. (George didn't demonstrate this; he claimed to be reformed after his Christian baptism.)

George's stories were so good (and apparently believable) that people in Europe demanded a book. So he wrote one, published in 1705, with the unbelievably long title of *An Historical and Geographical Description of Formosa: Giving an account of the religion, customs, manners, &c., of the inhabitants. Together with a relation of what happened to the author in his travels; particularly his conferences with the Jesuits, and others, in several parts of Europe. Also the history and reasons of his conversion to Christianity, with his*

CONNECTIONS

George Psalmanazar is an "expert" cited in a very famous work. That work is the essay "A Modest Proposal" by Jonathan Swift. Small world.

objections against it (in defence of Paganism) and their answers. George was nothing if not thorough in this book. He spoke in detail about cannibalism, human sacrifices, baby killing, and polygamy. He even included some grisly illustrations to drive home his point. The book was a huge success and was translated into multiple languages (not by George, of course). He became quite famous, in part because he was so believable, but also because people in Europe knew next to nothing about the world to the east. When George wrote about Formosan religion, culture, food, and clothes, nobody knew enough to contradict him.

Some people were suspicious of George, and they tried to trip him up in his lies. Edmund Halley, an astronomer in the Royal Society, famously tried to trick George by asking if the sun shone down the chimneys in Formosa, which is located in the tropics where the sun would be directly overhead at times. George slipped up and answered, no, the sun doesn't shine down chimneys. Edmund was delighted: "Aha!" he must have said. "You are a fake, sir!" George was quick on his feet, though. He quickly amended his statement. The chimneys in Formosa are twisted, he argued. And what could Edmund possibly say to that?

When other naysayers asked George why his skin was so white given that he claimed to be from a tropical island under Japanese control, he had a handy answer. He said that he spent his Formosa years in the shade or inside. Thus, his skin was not dark like people might expect. Again, people couldn't argue with him. How were they to know this wasn't true?

Far from being lazy, George didn't just make his living telling lies about Formosa. His day job involved writing books about printing. He was also a Hebrew scholar in his spare time. (No wonder he slept sitting up. He was too busy to lie down!) When his Formosa book became a runaway hit, Oxford College hired him to translate religious texts into Formosan language, the language that he completely made up. He did such a good job that Oxford asked him to teach Formosan to students. Imagine how stupid those students would have felt if they ever went to the island of Formosa. All they knew was George's gibberish.

George was such a successful faker because he had a rule he created and followed without exception. He called it his maxim: "Whatever I had once affirmed in conversation, tho' ever so improbably, or even absurd, should never be amended or contradicted." In other words, George stuck to his lies.

Though George became very famous and was sought after by people who wanted to ask him questions, learn from him, or try to trick him, he must have started to feel guilty because he confessed before he died. He arranged for a memoir confessing all his lies to be published after his death.

There was one thing he kept secret: his real name. To this day, nobody knows who George Psalmanazar really was. •

WASHINGTON IRVING

DATE: 1828

THE LIE: That Christopher Columbus was a whole lot smarter than he really was

REASON: To create a national hero

Every American kid learns about Christopher Columbus in school, but did you know that much of what we think we know about him isn't even true? You can thank someone named **Washington Irving** for that.

Washington was born in 1783, shortly after the Revolutionary War. His parents named him after the courageous war hero and first American president, General George Washington. They clearly expected big things from their son, and they were probably exceedingly proud that he grew up to become a lawyer. There was only one problem: He wasn't a very good lawyer. He barely passed the New York state bar exam, which is the difficult test all lawyers have to take. Washington was probably distracted because his real passion was writing comedy.

Can you imagine the conversation he must have had with his parents when he announced that dream?

> **Mr. Irving:** *Son, we named you after our revered first president because we knew you would go on to do great things, just like him.*
> **Mrs. Irving:** *We always knew you'd be as smart and serious and important as President Washington, sweetheart.*
> **Washington:** *Mom, Dad, I have something to tell you. I want to be a stand-up comedian. Knock-knock...*

Well, it wasn't exactly stand-up. That wasn't invented yet. But he did write comic essays and books under the very hilarious name Diedrich Knickerbocker. (Another pen name he used was the very fake-sounding Geoffrey Crayon.) In 1809, he wrote a humorous book called *Knickerbocker's History*

of New York. (You'll have to take my word for it that it was funny because Washington was evidently not very good at funny titles.)

You might know Washington for his short stories "Rip Van Winkle" and "The Legend of Sleepy Hollow." These stories became so popular that Washington is still known as one of the first and most famous American writers of fiction. The stories aren't really comic, but they do demonstrate Washington's big imagination.

Washington wasn't just a comedy and fiction writer. He also had a serious side, which was probably a relief to his parents. During his career, he wrote a biography about his namesake, George Washington. That biography was one of his biggest career achievements.

In addition to his writing, Washington served as the United States ambassador to Spain. Because of that job, he was hired to translate materials about Christopher Columbus. In Madrid, Washington became obsessed with Christopher and decided that he would write his own biography of Christopher and give him the credit Washington thought he was owed.

Christopher was in need of a good biographer, especially one like Washington who wasn't afraid to embellish the truth and tell outright lies if necessary. You see, Christopher — long dead, of course — was a bit of a laughingstock in Spain. Sure, he "discovered" America, but only by accident and not because he knew what he was doing. He sort of blundered upon the continent. Americans at the time barely remembered him. Washington figured that a really exciting biography was just the thing to save the reputation of a man who had died and been forgotten.

Washington got to work and painted Christopher as a hero who had God behind him. He turned Christopher into an underdog who triumphed over doubters, naysayers, and outright enemies who wanted to stop him from sailing. Washington transformed Christopher from a dope into a hero, all by the power of his pen. Check out this admiring paragraph from Washington's book, *A History of the Life and Voyages of Christopher Columbus*.

> It is the object of the following work to relate the deeds and fortunes of the mariner who first had the judgment to divine, and the intrepidity to brave the mysteries of this perilous deep, and who, by his hardy genius, his inflexible constancy, and his heroic courage, brought the ends of the earth into communication with each other.

Pretty high praise, right? It's sort of true. Christopher probably opened the door to trade between Europe and the Americas. But notice how Washington conveniently overlooks the disease Christopher unknowingly brought to the natives. And he doesn't even hint at the cruel behavior Christopher and his crew demonstrated, like the murdering of the natives who got in Christopher's way. These are not exactly small details, but Washington chose to overlook them.

Washington didn't just lie by omission. He told some outright falsehoods. The biggest lie Washington told about Christopher is one that persists today. You might have even learned this lie in one of your school textbooks. Washington wrote in his book that people in Christopher's time

BAD FOOD

Some medical researchers think Christopher Columbus died as a result of something called reactive arthritis, which is caused by intestinal bacteria. Another way of saying it is that Christopher Columbus died of food poisoning!

(the 1400s) believed the earth was flat. Christopher alone argued that it was round and set out to prove his countrymen wrong. That's a lie. A big fat one too. Educated people in Christopher's time knew very well that the earth was round. It had been an established fact for centuries. The Greeks knew it. Pythagoras (you might know him for his theorem) wrote about a spherical earth in the sixth century BC. And in the second century AD, Ptolemy wrote a book called the *Geography* about a round earth. Not only would Christopher have read it, but it was probably on his bookshelf.

But Washington needed to give Christopher something to fight for, something that would make him appear smarter than everyone else around him. So he wrote in his biography that brilliant Christopher taught the world that everyone was wrong about the flat earth. The lie is so engrained in our culture now that textbooks have reported it for years and years. There's actually a name for the lie: "The Flat Error." And it's all because Washington made up that story for his book.

Why would Washington tell such a lie? Well, he was concerned that Americans didn't have a legendary hero. He wanted America to have a strong history and cultural stories that would make us feel patriotic. He wanted us to have a symbol that would make us proud. Christopher seemed like the fellow to live in our memories. And he totally did, didn't he?

Whether Washington set out to lie or he was just a bad researcher is unclear. But what we do know is that Washington created a folk hero that endured for centuries. •

NEWSPAPER REPORTERS

DATE: 1923
THE LIE: That King Tut's tomb was cursed
REASON: To sell more papers

King Tut died in 1323 BC, when he was just nineteen, but it was thousands of years later before one dedicated explorer found his tomb. Howard Carter, an Englishman, went to Egypt in 1891 to look for undiscovered tombs. Ancient tomb raiders were common, so many Egyptian tombs had already been pillaged. Some people believed that all the tomb treasures were already gone. But Howard believed that there was still an undiscovered tomb.

Howard searched for years while being financed by a rich guy named George Edward Stanhope Molyneux Herbert, better known as Lord Carnarvon of England. When Howard found nothing after five years, Lord Carnarvon called him back to England to tell him that he was cutting off the funds. It seems like a strongly worded letter might have been a cheaper way to fire Howard, but meeting in person turned out to be a good thing. Howard was so persuasive that he convinced Lord Carnarvon to give him one last try to find the elusive tomb. So Howard went back to Egypt with money, supplies, and a yellow canary that he was sure would bring good luck.

On November 4, 1922, Howard and his team found King Tut's tomb. They immediately sent word back to England, and Lord Carnarvon arrived in Cairo on November 26 for the exciting tomb-opening event. Inside the tomb, the team found King Tut's mummy and lots of treasures, exactly as Howard predicted. The real excitement didn't start until a bit later though.

Just two months after Howard and his team unsealed the inner chamber, Lord Carnarvon died. Newspapers began reporting all kinds of crazy events that they associated with the opening of the tomb. The events were coincidences that were easily explainable, but that didn't stop the reporters from turning these coincidences into spooky events. For instance, the lights went out in Cairo when the team opened the tomb, which reporters speculated signaled the release of the curse. The reality was that the power went off in Cairo all the time in the 1920s. People claimed that a cobra ate Howard's yellow canary the day he found the tomb. The reality was that the canary was given to a friend (who was a human, not a cobra).

Many people believed that ancient mummy powder had mystical powers that killed Lord Carnarvon in retaliation for disturbing the tomb and the sarcophagus. The truth is that Lord Carnarvon got a mosquito bite on his cheek, which he later cut while shaving. The open sore became infected, and he died as a result. It didn't help that he was already in poor health and there weren't antibiotics to help him fight the infection. The official cause

TWO BAD MUMMY JOKES

Q: What brand of underwear do mummies wear?
A: *Fruit of the Tomb*

Q: Where do mummies swim?
A: *In the Dead Sea*

TEN MUMMY FACTS

1. Egyptians removed the lungs, liver, stomach, and intestines from dead bodies to keep the mummy from rotting.
2. South Americans were mummifying bodies before the Egyptians did.
3. It took about seventy days to mummify a body properly. It also required three people: an embalmer, a cutter, and a scribe. (The scribe sounds like the easiest and cleanest job.)
4. Tomb raiders were common, so mummies frequently had to be rewrapped or relocated.
5. Anyone could be mummified if that person had enough money.
6. Mummies often wore wigs.
7. There's a god of mummification. His name is Anubis.
8. Even animals were sometimes mummified.
9. People wanted to be mummified because it preserved the body for use in the afterlife. (And that wig probably came in handy in the afterlife.)
10. King Tut had six chariots with him in his tomb. (He also had zero cavities in his teeth.)

of death is blood poisoning, not an uncommon disease at the time. (Can you imagine? Dying from a mosquito bite and a shaving cut? That's far less exciting than dying of an ancient curse.)

The story of King Tut's curse might have died shortly after Lord Carnarvon except for two things: First, when King Tut's mummy was unwrapped in 1925, it was reported that King Tut had a cut on his cheek in the same place as Lord Carnarvon's deadly mosquito bite. Second, other people from the tomb excavation started dropping dead. By 1935, the media reported that twenty-one people from the team had died since the opening of the tomb.

The media reported on King Tut's curse so much that many people today still believe King Tut's tomb was cursed. Debunkers have pointed out that while many people on the team did die, the majority didn't. Howard, the head tomb raider, lived to the relatively ripe age of sixty-four and died of lymphoma, which is a deadly type of cancer. It's hard to believe an ancient curse took the form of a slow-moving cancer.

Some people argued that maybe the dust from the mummy might have included bacteria spores. Maybe virulent bacteria slowly killed the tomb raiders. But that explanation has been debunked as well. Some scientists say that the air was probably healthier inside the tomb than outside it, given that Cairo in the 1920s was teeming with disease and bacteria that Lord Carnarvon, Howard, and the rest of the team would have been breathing every single day.

Still, the media reported on King Tut's curse every time a team member died, no matter what the actual cause of death. Can you guess why? Yup, you are right. King Tut's curse sold a lot of newspapers. The curse proves that sometimes lying can make a few people a whole lot of money. •

CHAPTER 3:
HORSEPLAY

THE ANCIENT GREEKS

DATE: A very, very long time ago
THE LIE: That a giant horse was a parting gift to the gods
REASON: To destroy the city of Troy

Way back between 1200 and 601 BC, a poet was born. His name was **Homer**, and he is still considered one of the most influential writers of all time. Ironically, he never actually wrote anything. Instead, he told stories that later became *The Iliad* and *The Odyssey*. These stories were eventually written down by a number of different writers, but Homer gets the credit for them even today.

A story from *The Iliad* represents one of the biggest lies ever told. It's the story of the **Trojan horse**. The Greeks and the Trojans were in an epic war that had already lasted ten years. The war began because of a Greek woman named Helen. She was the most beautiful woman in the world; in fact, she had a "face that launched a thousand ships." Helen proves that it's tough being beautiful. An epic war was fought over her!

You can blame Paris for what happened next. He was a handsome young man from Troy who either seduced Helen or kidnapped her from her crusty old husband. Either way, she left Greece and sailed to Troy. Her husband was pretty angry — angry enough to go to war with an entire country. Oh, and by the way, Helen was the daughter of Zeus, so you can see why Paris's crime was a pretty big deal.

After years of fighting, the Greeks came up with a great idea: They built a giant wooden horse that they offered to the people of Troy. Then they sailed away to a nearby island to wait and watch. The Trojans assumed that the Greeks were surrendering. Sinon, a clever Greek soldier, told the Trojans to take the horse because the goddess Athena wanted them to have it. She would keep them safe. The Trojans apparently thought that was a perfectly logical explanation. Why wouldn't a goddess send them a massive wooden horse as a good luck charm? (Times have changed. Can you imagine anyone now thinking that a mammoth horse statue on wheels is a fine gift?)

A Nervous Nellie from Troy named Cassandra warned that the horse was a trick, but nobody listened to her. (To do this day, being a "Cassandra" means that you foresee doom, but nobody believes you. She's sort of a reverse Boy-Who-Cried-Wolf.) A smart Trojan soldier named Laocoön was also pretty sure that bringing the horse behind the walls of Troy was a mega-bad idea. But after he warned everyone, he and his sons were killed by serpents from the sea. And the residents of Troy figured that was a pretty clear sign from Athena and the gods that they better take the horse.

So the residents of Troy brought the large, wheeled equine into the fortified city. From there, they did what every group of humans would do after a hard decade of war: They got really, really drunk.

Once the Trojans passed out or fell asleep from all the partying, the Greeks made their move. You see, the wooden horse was full of Greek soldiers just waiting to pounce on the unsuspecting Trojans. It was a bloody battle, and not many Trojans survived.

The Greeks were pretty proud of themselves for coming up with such a masterful lie. To be fair, all the credit really goes to Odysseus. He's the guy who came up with the idea in the first place, but he apparently lacked carpentry skills. Epeus, a skilled carpenter, was summoned to build the thing. And all those Greek soldiers had to be perfectly quiet for hours until the time was right to pop out and begin the massacre. Imagine if you had to pee while stuck inside that giant wooden horse!

CITIES OF TROY

Troy was located in what we now know as Turkey. It didn't survive, but other cities named Troy are alive and well. Just in the United States, there are Troys in New York, New Hampshire, Missouri, Ohio, Illinois, Michigan, Alabama, North Carolina, and Texas.

SICK HORSES

A *Trojan horse* doesn't always refer to a giant wooden statue. A Trojan virus is a kind of malware that can infect your computer. A Trojan horse can trick you into installing programs that have viruses because the application looks harmless or like something you would want. Once you install it, the virus is free to replicate all over your computer. Imagine little computer Greeks climbing out of a horse and wreaking havoc on your system.

One Trojan virus of special note is an unofficial (read: infected) version of the *Angry Birds Space* smartphone game. It looks just like the real *Angry Birds* product, but it's real purpose is to install bad code into your smartphone. So beware (and only use online marketplaces that you can trust.).

The story of the Trojan horse is most accurately classified as a literary lie. The event probably didn't really happen, but the story helps us understand the culture, values, and happenings of people thousands of years ago. Twenty-seven centuries ago, when Homer first told the story, people believed it was a real. They listened with rapt interest as Homer detailed the Greeks' ingenious plan. They were particularly interested because they believed their ancestors were part of this epic war. The story helped them feel connected to their past.

Not only does the Trojan horse story give us a tiny window into what life was like between 1200 and 900 BC, but it teaches us a valuable lesson about accepting gifts from our enemies. You might have heard the expression "Beware of Greeks bearing gifts." Well, the Trojan horse is where that expression came from.

Homer may have been telling stories thousands of years ago, but his lessons are still relevant: People lie, so be suspicious. Especially if those people are offering you a gift horse. •

CLEVER HANS

DATE: 1891
THE LIE: That he could do math
REASON: Because he wanted to please people

Everyone thinks his or her pet is smart, but be honest: Can yours do math? Wilhelm von Osten of Germany believed that his horse, Kluge Hans (which translates to **Clever Hans**), could solve math equations. Wilhelm would ask Hans questions, and then Hans would tap a hoof to answer. For instance, if Wilhelm asked what the square root of four is, Hans would tap twice. Hans could even do fractions, tapping out the numerator and denominator. Later, Hans learned to spell names, tell time, and identify dates.

Wilhelm, a retired schoolteacher, was so understandably impressed with Hans that he took Hans all over Germany to show him off. Everyone wanted to meet the world's smartest horse, and as a result, man and horse became quite famous. The *New York Times* even ran a story about Hans on the front page.

Wilhelm was ecstatic because he could finally prove what he'd always believed to be true: Animals are just as smart as humans. He felt pretty lucky to have found Hans, an Arab stallion from Russia. Before Hans, Wilhelm tried to train a cat and a bear to do math. Both animals were dismally bad at it. You can imagine how excited Wilhelm was to find a willing pupil. You can also imagine how difficult it must have been to try to teach a bear. Don't you wonder how he went about that task?

Wilhelm was convinced that Hans was a genius horse and boldly welcomed anyone to investigate his training methods. People were flummoxed by Hans and his impressive grasp of math and put together a Hans Commission to study the horse. The commission was made up of teachers, zoologists, animal trainers, and even a circus manager. After months of study, the committee definitively ruled that Wilhelm was not lying and that Hans really could do math. One mathematician admitted that Hans had the math ability of a fourteen-year-old boy. (Mental note: Hire horse as algebra tutor.)

A man named Oskar Pfungst, a German biologist and psychologist, remained skeptical. It was Oskar who finally figured out what was really happening. Hans couldn't do math. He didn't know any more math than your gerbil or your goldfish. Hans was lying! Not intentionally, of course. He was a horse. But what Hans was doing was responding to subtle visual cues given by humans. He was trying to please his masters without knowing what he was doing!

Once Oskar figured that out, he decided to try an experiment. Oskar placed Hans behind a screen so he couldn't see any humans. Without subtle

GRIMM TALE

"Clever Hans" is actually the name of a fairy tale by Jacob and Wilhelm Grimm. In the story, Hans (who is not a horse) finds himself engaged to Gretel. Every morning he asks her for a gift. She gives him all kinds of strange things, including a goat, a calf, a ham, and finally herself. Each time he receives a gift, he does something stupid with it because apparently Hans is an utter moron. For example, he tries to lead the ham around on a leash until a dog eats it. And he pokes out the eyes of the calf.

By the end of the story, Hans loses his bride because he's such an idiot. The title is meant to be ironic because Hans is anything but clever. The moral of the story seems to be that girls should beware of dumb boys.

cues from humans, Hans didn't know the answers to the questions. And when the humans didn't know the answers to the questions, Hans couldn't accurately answer. The only reason Hans was able to correctly answer questions was by "reading" the people in the room.

Because of Hans, we now know that some animals, including horses, can detect tension or even heartbeats. They often pick up on visual cues so subtle that humans don't notice them. But Hans was very aware of everyone and everything happening in the room. When he sensed that he was supposed to stop tapping his hoof, he did. And when he was right, he got a lot of praise. Hans wasn't so much a liar as a good-natured pleaser. The people in the room, including Wilhelm, were answering their own questions by giving the answers to Hans.

All of Hans's training was worthwhile, even if it didn't prove that horses could do math. For one thing, it taught humans that animals are excellent readers of unconscious physical cues. That alone is still impressive. (And it explains why your dog seems to know what to do when you are sad or happy or just in need of a good cuddle.)

Hans also helped psychologists study what is now called the Clever Hans Phenomenon. It's the study of unconscious cuing, sometimes called ideomotor reaction. Oskar got so good at it that he was able to give correct answers even when he didn't know the questions — all by reading the audience just as Hans did. Oskar got smarter by studying a horse.

Clever Hans wasn't a genius, but he was a pretty smart horse, and he managed to fool a lot of smart people for a long time with his not-quite-a-lie. That alone is worth a spot in the pantheon of the world's greatest horses. •

CHAPTER 4:
STINKIN' STORIES

THE LIAR:

HENRY LOUIS MENCKEN

DATE: December 28, 1917

THE LIE: That Millard Fillmore had a bathtub installed in the White House in 1851

REASON: Because he was feeling depressed about World War I

Henry Louis (H.L.) Mencken was a journalist who wrote prolifically on just about every subject you can imagine — from religion to chiropractic medicine. One of his most famous pieces was a short essay he wrote for the *New York Evening Mail*. "A Neglected Anniversary" was published on December 28, 1917, and on the surface, the essay seems kind of boring. It was about the history of the bathtub. Specifically, H.L. lamented that our country let December 20 pass by without celebrating the seventy-fifth anniversary of one of our favorite household fixtures: the tub. In the essay, he informed readers that there was a party planned (who wouldn't want to attend a surprise party on behalf of bathtubs?), but it was canceled when alcohol prohibition laws got in the way. Apparently people decided you couldn't celebrate a bathtub birthday without champagne and wine coolers.

H.L. was presumably the lone person who commemorated the bathtub's big day. His column went on to detail a pretty fascinating history of the bathtub. He talked about people from the past who originally thought bathing was a health risk. Some of these people were doctors. Can you imagine your doctor telling you to avoid bathing?

According to H.L.'s article, the bathtub might have gone down as a totally useless invention if not for President Millard Fillmore, who had one installed in the White House in 1851. Suddenly, everyone in America wanted a bathtub; it was considered a "monarchical" luxury. And who wouldn't want to have kingly accessories?

I'm positive that you have a bathtub in your house (and maybe even more than one). According to H.L., you have Millard Fillmore and the geniuses who invented a rectangular receptacle for water to thank.

MILLARD FILLMORE, OUR THIRTEENTH PRESIDENT

Millard Fillmore was technically not elected president. He was Zachary Taylor's vice-president. A reluctant member of the Whig Party, Zachary was wealthy, brave, and resourceful, but he was also crude and often disheveled. Millard was handsome and athletic, a nice balance to Zachary.

Zachary was a celebrated Mexican War hero who refused to take a position on slavery when he was the Democratic candidate for president. Because he tried to please both pro- and anti-slavery voters, Zachary appealed to everyone. But he was actually very opposed to slavery and might have changed the course of history if he hadn't died sixteen months into his term.

Zachary was a hero on the battlefield, but he did not die a heroic death. On July 4, 1850, Zachary went to a Fourth of July party where he enjoyed cold milk and fresh cherries. Soon after, he got sick. Five days later, he died. There is still debate among scholars and historians about how he died. It might have been food poisoning or cholera.

With Zachary dead, Millard Fillmore became president. He had no notable accomplishments, and when the time came for another election, his party selected a war hero named Winfield Scott. (He lost to Franklin Pierce.)

Poor Millard's greatest accomplishment seems to have been the installation of the bathtub — and that never even happened!

But wait! Don't mark December 20 on your calendar as a key day in history. It turns out that H.L. was lying. He made up the whole story about the bathtub's birthday and Fillmore installing one in the White House. H.L. meant for his essay to be satirical. Nothing in the article about the history of the bathtub was even a little bit true.

Once H.L. admitted he lied, the whole story should have been over. The problem was that journalists kept reporting it. Not three weeks after H.L.'s original essay, the *Boston Herald* printed the same story as factual. Not surprisingly, readers figured it must be true. (Some people even claimed they could corroborate the story.)

So many people repeated the lie over the course of the next eight years that H.L. was forced to write a retraction to convince people that his essay was a satire. But it didn't matter. People still believed it. That's because other publications and reference books were still reporting H.L.'s story as fact. H.L. published another retraction, begging people to recognize that he was just telling a joke. He had no luck. People still believed his bathtub lies.

To this day, some encyclopedias still repeat H.L.'s story about Millard Fillmore's bathtub as fact. White House tour guides sometimes falsely report that President Fillmore popularized bathing in America. Trivia games have included questions about the president responsible for installing the first tub. Even the *Washington Post*, a reputable newspaper, fell victim to H.L.'s column: It printed H.L.'s "facts" about the bathtub in 2004 and was forced to apologize when astute readers called it out.

People who hated doctors liked H.L.'s essay because they could use it to "prove" that doctors were stupid. After all, what kind of moron would believe that bathing is bad for the body?

That so many people repeated the story incensed H.L. He argued that such sloppy reporting was evidence of how lazy American journalists had become. If we couldn't even trust what they reported on bathtubs, could we really trust what they were saying about World War I? The whole incident proved to H.L. that "most of the so-called knowledge of humanity" is garbage — or what he called "buncombe."

You might be wondering why H.L. would make up such a ridiculous story in the first place. When asked, H.L. said it was just "a piece of spoofing to relieve the strain of war days." Given how little faith he had in journalists (even though he was one), the story might have been a test. If that's the case, America's media failed miserably. H.L. even planted some clues that the story was a hoax. He cited journals that nobody could find. That alone should have stopped anyone from reporting his story; instead, other reporters proved that H.L. was right when he argued that history is just "bunk."

H.L.'s bathtub story is one of the greatest media hoaxes of all time. The town of Moravia, New York, celebrates it in a weird way. Every year, the town hosts Fillmore Days. It's a giant festival with food, fun, and games. What's the most popular game? Well, bathtub races, of course! •

ADVERTISERS FOR LISTERINE

DATE: 1920s
THE LIE: That bad breath was a medical problem
REASON: To sell mouthwash

Nobody likes having bad breath. Probably the only thing worse than having bad breath is being around someone else who has it. Savvy **advertisers for Listerine** figured out how to capitalize on people's fear of bad breath. Their campaign was so successful that Listerine is still a popular mouth hygiene product. But did you know that these clever marketers sold a fake affliction that could only be "cured" with what was originally a disinfectant?

Listerine was invented by two doctors, Nicole Dyer Lawrence and Christian Bach, in 1879 for Lambert Pharmaceutical Company. The product was used as an antiseptic for surgery; in fact, it later saved many soldiers' lives in World War I. Imagine having your doctor enter the operating room with a scalpel and a bottle of mouthwash!

The product was named after Dr. Joseph Lister, who figured out that pouring the stuff on wounds fought bacteria and infections. Other doctors realized that Listerine could do all kinds of amazing things. Since its invention, it's been used to successfully treat gonorrhea (a sexually transmitted disease), wash floors, eradicate dandruff, fight colds, prevent armpit odor, clean teeth, and attack acne. That's a lot of uses for one product, right? You could clear out your medicine chest and fill it with Listerine.

In the early 1920s, a team of executives decided that Listerine needed some targeted advertising to keep the liquid moving off the shelves. Milton Feasley, Gordon Seagrave, and Gerard B. Lambert wanted to sell Listerine as mouthwash, an emerging market, but that was a tough sell. At that time, people didn't think they needed such a product. Bad breath was just a fact of life, like having boogers in your nose or expelling gas from your behind. Nobody likes it, but it happens and there's not much you can do about it. Not so, said these men. They set out to convince people that bad breath was

CREATIVE USES FOR MOUTHWASH

Sugarless mouthwash is great for freshening your breath if you don't have time to brush, but you can use mouthwash for all kinds of other things.

- It's an excellent antiseptic — pour it on your cuts to hasten healing, but expect it to burn a little.
- It can clean glass.
- It disinfects — go ahead, wash your toilet with it.
- It's a deodorant — use cotton balls to dab it under your armpits.
- It's a detergent — drop a capful in your washing machine.
- It's a dandruff shampoo — wash your hair and then pour a little mouthwash over your head.

a medical condition, something in need of a strong antibiotic solution that would attack mouth germs like a battalion of tiny armed soldiers. That's when the men came up with the problem of halitosis.

Halitosis is a Latin word that means "unpleasant breath," but these brilliant advertisers decided to present halitosis to the public as a serious medical problem, one that required a medicine as strong as Listerine. (Remember that Listerine had previously been used to clean open wounds and disinfect floors. It isn't exactly a wimpy substance. Using Listerine for bad breath is a little bit like cutting toothpicks with a chainsaw.)

The ad men worried at first that talking about such a personal hygiene problem would be vulgar, but it turned out that America was ready and willing to talk about bad breath. Americans were desperately afraid of having any health problems, especially ones related to foul breath. The Listerine ads made people stop thinking of bad breath as an unfortunate consequence of being human; instead, people began to think of it as a disease. See what the advertisers did there? They convinced the public that something perfectly normal was actually an illness — an illness that required a product to cure.

The ad campaign was brilliant. One of the first and most famous ads shows a happy couple with a sad, shameful single lady in the corner. The ad copy tells readers, "Halitosis makes you unpopular." In small print, the ad says, "Don't fool yourself. Since halitosis never announces itself, to the victim, you simply cannot know when you have it." The ad suggests that the single lady wouldn't be single if she could just get her bad breath under control.

In another ad, the copy warns, "You can lose him in a minute." The ad shows a handsome man paying attention to a woman other than his girlfriend. Presumably, the girlfriend has dragon breath, but the other woman has breath as fresh as a daisy. Another ad features a cute girl named Patty who "gets her prince" after she gets Listerine. One print ad presents Edna, "often a bridesmaid, but never a bride." Poor Edna is single and nearing the "tragic" age of thirty, all because of her foul breath. One of the most offensive and unintentionally hilarious ads suggests that women with halitosis should wear a bell around their necks to signal their horrifying smell.

Are you seeing any recurring themes here? That's right. All the ads feature women who can't get or keep a date because of their bad breath. It's not that men have great breath in the morning. The ads targeted women because that's who did the shopping.

But Listerine was not above exploiting men's fears. The marketing campaigns aimed at dudes suggested they use Listerine to treat dandruff. A popular Listerine ad shows a disgusted women wiping dandruff from a man's shoulder. "Why Frank," she's saying with exasperation, as if she spends her whole life sweeping white flakes from her husband's shoulders. Listerine was also targeted at men with germ problems. One ad guarantees the product could kill 200 million germs in just fifteen seconds. And in case you were wondering where these germs were, rest assured, the ad says, "it may be used in any body cavity." (I think we can all agree that's alarming. What other cavities besides your mouth would one want to put this stuff in?)

The halitosis campaign was so successful that Listerine went from making a measly $100,000 in 1921 to an impressive $4,000,000 in 1927. Other advertisers took note and tried to come up with other impressive-sounding

WEIRD TOOTHPASTE FLAVORS

Mouthwash is usually minty, but toothpaste doesn't have to be. Check out these flavors of toothpaste. These actually exist!

- Chocolate
- Bacon
- Ice cream
- Whiskey
- Licorice
- Charcoal
- Champagne

maladies. For example, bromodosis is an affliction of smelly feet. Acidosis is a stomachache. Homotosis is the very serious disease of having ugly furniture. (Surprisingly, Listerine was not used to treat any of these "diseases.")

The "halitosis appeal" represents a kind of advertising technique called sociodrama. Ad men figured out that Listerine wasn't very exciting simply as a product. But once they tied it to a story — like Edna's, or Patty's, or Frank and his flaky scalp — they could sell their audience a lifestyle. Audiences believed that Listerine would cure their breath and usher Prince Charming right through the front door. (Undoubtedly Prince Charming would also have to use Listerine in his various body cavities.)

Listerine does work on bad breath, by the way. If you wake up with morning breath, as every human does, a mouthful of Listerine will clear it right up. You know what else will do that? Any other kind of mouthwash or just a good teeth-brushing. Some dental research suggests that going to the dentist twice a year and brushing and flossing twice daily are far more important than mouthwash (and will help keep bad breath at bay).

In 2005, a federal judge ordered Listerine, owned at the time by Pfizer, to stop claiming Listerine was as effective as flossing. It's not. Sorry. Your mom is right, as usual. You do have to brush and floss your teeth twice a day! •

YOUTUBE USER "AHSCOTTY"

DATE: October 2010

THE LIE: That a Japanese scientist was making steaks out of poop

REASON: Nobody knows

You might want to skip this section if you have a weak stomach.

In 2011 FoxNews.com reported a truly disgusting story: Mitsuyuki Ikeda, a Japanese scientist, had found a way to recycle feces into supposedly delicious poop burgers. As the story goes, Mitsuyuki was working for Okayama Laboratory in Japan when Tokyo Sewage approached him with a problem: They had too much sewage sludge. (It's hard to imagine that a place called Tokyo Sewage could have too much of the stuff.) A normal person would have said, "Sorry you have too much poop, but I'm not sure what you want me to do about it." Not Mitsuyuki. He studied the sewage and decided that there must be something interesting he could do with all that protein teeming in the bacteria.

FoxNews.com reported that Mitsuyuki figured that protein is an essential part of our diet, so why not turn poop into food? Totally logical. I mean, lots of people in the world are starving. If we could turn poop into food, we'd never have a food shortage again. Even the vegetarians among us can partake of the poop without murder on their conscience. Brilliant. Give this guy a Nobel Prize immediately, right? Wrong. Keep reading.

According to the original news story, Mitsuyuki figured out how to separate the yummy protein from most of the gross stuff using a machine called an exploder. What emerged from his exploder was a meat-like substance that's more than 50 percent protein but also more than 40 percent rat, mouse, and human poop with some toilet paper seasoning. Mitsuyuki added some soy flavoring and some red food coloring, and there you have it: a very delicious poop steak.

As with any new creation, there are some problems. One is that, in spite of Mitsuyuki's awesome exploder technology, turd burgers were ten to twenty times more expensive than what you and I can buy at the grocery store or a restaurant. Second, in case you've forgotten, the burgers are made out of poop, so there's that potential marketing problem. The third — and most certainly the biggest — problem is that the whole thing was a hoax.

After FoxNews.com ran the story in its Science section, other media outlets picked up the story. It's appeared everywhere from the *Guardian*, a respected publication in the United Kingdom, to *LA Weekly* and Discovery.com, just to name three. Suddenly, everyone was talking about edible poop.

A reporter named Justin Elliott from Salon.com got suspicious and started investigating this story. He uncovered something very surprising. FoxNews had gotten all its information from a YouTube video, posted by a user named "**ahscotty**" in October of 2010. Eight months later, FoxNews posted the story on its site. Then all the other media outlets jumped on board. Nobody bothered to fact-check the information presented in this YouTube video (which, I must admit, does seem very convincing).

Justin decided to track down the Okayama Laboratory where the video was supposedly shot and where Mitsuyuki kept his fascinating exploder machine. The laboratory does exist, but nobody there knew anything about poop-to-food conversion. Okayama Laboratory makes stents, a kind of medical device. Furthermore, the lab didn't employ Mitsuyuki, though a Mitsuyuki Ikeda does exist. He's the director of the Okayama UNESCO Association, and he looks an awful lot like the guy in the video, only older. When Justin from Salon.com emailed Mitsuyuki to ask if he created the video, Mitsuyuki did not respond. And he hasn't responded to any of the other curious reporters or YouTube viewers who want to know why anyone would make and post this very strange video.

The video itself seems professional. It shows a man working in a lab with lots of fancy-looking equipment. The video is narrated by a smart-sounding British man who explains exactly how poop becomes burgers that are then served in a restaurant. (Justin, the skeptical reporter, points out that the restaurant sign shown in the video uses Chinese characters, not Japanese.) The British narrator points out that poop meat has far fewer calories than real meat. I guess that's helpful information for anyone who wants to snarf down some turds without jeopardizing a low-cal diet.

My favorite part of the video is the pointer the scientist uses to high-light information on a flowchart. The wooden pointer has a rubber hand stuck on the end of it, and the rubber hand has one red-nailed finger that

FOURTEEN INTERESTING POOP FACTS

1. Poop is mostly made of water.
2. Poop comes in many colors besides brown — it can be yellow, black, red, green, or white.
3. The word *poop* comes from the Middle English word *poupen*, which means "fart."
4. *Poupen* sounds like a fart, which is how the word came about.
5. People started using the word *poop* in about 1900.
6. Coprophagia is a real disease — people who have it eat poop.
7. If your poop floats, it means it has a lot of gas in it.
8. The longest measured poop was twenty-six feet long.
9. Poop is smelly because of all the bacteria in it.
10. Eating meat makes your poop smellier.
11. Most adult humans poop about two pounds a day.
12. Elephants poop eighty pounds a day.
13. Parasites called pinworms live in your butt.
14. The British invented an explosive that looked like a poop.

he uses to emphasize key moments in the poop conversion process as it is illustrated on laminated visual aids. The whole video clip is overlaid with Asian-infused music, the kind you might hear at a Chinese restaurant in any American suburb.

Watching the video gives one the sense that someone took a lot of time and care to make this video seem as convincing as possible. But why? What would be the benefit of convincing people that a poop burger exists? That's a question that nobody has been able to answer.

What's even more surprising is that poop burger hoaxes are nothing new. A quick search in a newspaper database shows that the same basic story was reported in the 1990s. That led Justin and other skeptics to speculate that maybe Mitsuyuki made this video when he was younger and now wants nothing to do with it. Since he hasn't denied it, we are simply left to guess whether or not he was involved in the video or if someone just borrowed his name.

Some papers and websites printed retractions and apologies once Justin pointed out that absolutely no evidence exists to support the poop burger story. Interestingly, the story is still on the FoxNews website under the Food & Drink heading.

The hoax does point to some serious problems with our news media. If our sources of information are taking their information from YouTube, then we have a real problem, one that needs to be addressed.

Some people still want to believe that the poop burger is a real thing, but if it is, no real person has found any evidence of a lab or a scientist who has created such a thing.

If you want to eat poop, it looks like you'll have to do it the old-fashioned way. But I wouldn't recommend it. •

GREAT PRETENDERS

Throughout history, lots of liars pretended to be people they were not. In many cases, they made tons of money or became very famous because of their masquerades. In other cases, people pretended in order to call attention to important causes or to do things they couldn't do as themselves.

We've all probably pretended to be something we are not, but I'm willing to bet none of us has ever pulled off an identity disguise like the people in this chapter.

Before you get started reading, take this quiz to find out if your pretending has ever reached the heights of the pretending the folks in this chapter did.

HOW BIG OF A PRETENDER ARE YOU?

Answer the following questions with "yes" or "no."

1. Have you ever pretended to be a freed slave?
2. Have you ever written a play and pretended Shakespeare wrote it instead of you?
3. Have you ever pretended to be an airline pilot?
4. Have you ever lip-synched a song and told everyone it was really you singing?
5. Have you ever written a memoir pretending you were a criminal?
6. Have you ever created an online persona that was nothing like your real identity?
7. Have you ever pretended to be a descendent of a very rich man?
8. Have you ever pretended to be a descendent of a royal family?
9. Have you ever pretended to be a man in order to board a pirate ship?
10. Have you ever pretended to be a man in order to fight in a war?
11. Have you ever pretended to be an old woman to write an advice column?
12. Have you ever pretended to be a middle-aged man?

If you answered **no** to all of these questions, congratulate yourself. You are not a pretender. You are happy just being you. If you want to board a pirate ship, you'll do it as yourself, thank you very much.

If you answered **yes** to any of these questions, you might be a great pretender. You have a lot in common with the pretenders in this chapter. Some are historical heroes. Others are dead, disgraced, or both. And many spent time in jail.

If you're a great pretender, you might want to think about turning your life around now while there's still time. •

CHAPTER 5:
FAKERS

MATTIE GRIFFITH

DATE: 1856

THE LIE: That she was an escaped slave

REASON: To raise money to free her own slaves

Martha "Mattie" Griffith was born in Kentucky in about 1825 (nobody knows the date for sure) to Thomas and Catherine Griffith. Tragically, Thomas and Catherine died before Mattie was five years old. After their deaths, she inherited some land and six slaves. Mattie, however, was adamantly opposed to slavery. You might think that she could have just freed her slaves, but it wasn't that simple. First of all, she had to be old enough to do it. Second, she needed money to keep her land without slaves. Third, and most important, she needed money to transport her slaves to Ohio and get them started in a new life. If she just freed them, they wouldn't have anywhere to go.

Thoroughly disgusted with slavery in Kentucky and her inability to free her slaves, Mattie eventually moved to Philadelphia to live with her sister and her family, who were very poor. While in Philadelphia, Mattie converted from Catholicism to Protestantism because her priest advised her not to free her slaves.

Even far away from her home, Mattie didn't forget about her slaves in Kentucky. She came up with an idea that would involve lying, but Mattie was desperate to get money to free her slaves and fight for abolition. She would try anything. She decided to write an "autobiography" from the perspective of a freed slave. Keep in mind that Mattie was white and had never been a slave, but she wrote convincingly and eventually published her book, *Autobiography of a Female Slave.*

In the book, Mattie presents herself as a former slave named Ann who encounters all kinds of horrible events. Ann is whipped, abused, and threatened by her different masters. Ann eventually finds true love in Henry, but he kills himself after their attempts to buy their freedom are thwarted by Ann's nemesis, another slave named Lindy. At the end of the book, Ann is freed in her mistress's will. She moves north and teaches children for the rest of her life. Ann implores readers just to say no to slavery.

THIRTEEN FACTS ABOUT SLAVERY

1. In Africa, before the slave trade began, treating slaves well was important for developing a good reputation in a community.
2. Slavery started in Virginia in 1654.
3. Approximately 12.5 million Africans (a quarter of whom were children) were loaded on ships bound for the Americas. About 10.5 million people survived the difficult trip.
4. The first recorded slaveholder in the United States was a black man.
5. The invention of the cotton gin inadvertently increased slavery. More farmers were planting cotton crops, which required a cheap workforce.
6. Almost half of all slaves in the United States worked in cotton fields.
7. Cotton slaves worked about 3,000 or 4,000 hours a year. That's about eight or ten hours a day of hard labor every single day of the year
8. Slave mothers in the United States had about ten kids on average.
9. By 1860, 89 percent of all black people in the United States were slaves.
10. In 1860, 90 percent of slaves did not live past the age of fifty. Even worse, almost 98 percent did not live past the age of sixty.
11. Because of poor nutrition and horrific working conditions, enslaved black people were generally shorter than white people.
12. Enslaved children were expected to start working at age three or four.
13. Some experts suggest that there is more slavery now than at any other time in history. Around the world, an estimated 27 million people are enslaved right now.

Mattie's book was a hit, in part because slave narratives were extremely popular at the time. Many freed slaves, like Frederick Douglass, wrote accounts of their lives. Other slaves who couldn't write traveled around and told stories about their years in captivity. There were so many slave narratives published that the form influenced American literature forever. From 1760 to 1865, more than 100 slave autobiographies were published, including Mattie's.

Like the autobiographies before hers, Mattie's book was intended to show people the horrible lives slaves were forced to live. Mattie knew lying was bad, but she did it because she wanted readers to know just how inhumane and morally wrong slavery really was. Pretending to be black and a freed slave gave her authority she didn't think she could have demonstrated as a white woman writing about slavery.

You might be surprised to know that pretending to be someone from another race to write books was fairly common in Mattie's time. There is even a name for it now: "ethnic transvestism."

Mattie's book was so convincing that William Lloyd Garrison, a famous supporter of abolition, reviewed the book and was amazed at Ann's story. The fact that he noticed her book gave her lots of free publicity. Imagine if Oprah had read it. That's sort of what William's endorsement was like.

Mattie felt guilty about lying though, so a few months after the book came out, she admitted that she lied. She said she simply told stories based on facts she had heard or experienced.

In the end, the book wasn't a financial success. A few people read it, but not enough to help Mattie earn the kind of money she needed. Maybe it would have made more money if she hadn't have admitted her ruse, but she did and many people were shocked that a nice white woman from the north would write such horrible things about slavery, even if they were true.

Poor Mattie was abandoned by many of her friends, who thought she was ridiculous for having pulled such a stunt. Many of these friends were ardent believers in slavery, and Mattie would not stay quiet about her beliefs.

It was good that Mattie was loud though, because the American Anti-Slavery Society finally gave her the money to go back to Kentucky to free her slaves. She granted their emancipation and moved them to Ohio to live freely.

Mattie's story ends happily too. At the age of forty-one, she married for the first time. She and her husband became vocal supporters of women's voting rights and were strong supporters for abolition causes until their deaths. Mattie didn't die until 1906, so she got to see all the slaves freed in her lifetime. Imagine how happy she was.

FREDERICK DOUGLASS, CLEVER BOY

Frederick Douglass was an extraordinary man who escaped slavery. He learned to read as a child by cleverly challenging schoolboys to write letters in the dirt. That's how he learned the basics of reading and writing.

After he fought his way to freedom, he became the first black man to hold a high-ranking position in the United States government. He even ran for vice-president in 1872. His running mate was Victoria Woodhull, and their platform was equal rights for women and black people.

EARLY SLAVE NARRATIVES

One of the first slave autobiographies was the best seller *The Interesting Narrative of the Life of Olaudah Equiano; or, Gustavus Vassa, the African. Written by Himself.* It was published in 1789, and it was about the life of a man sold into slavery in West Africa who escaped to England to be free.

Recent evidence suggests that the writer was never a slave and was born in North America. Nevertheless, Olaudah's autobiography presented the horrors of slave trips and made many readers re-think their position on slavery in America.

Until the day she died, Mattie was known as a free spirit, someone who wasn't shy about speaking loudly and proudly about causes in which she believed strongly. She was also well known for dressing in all red. Even her gloves were red.

Mattie Griffith may not have made a lot of money on her book, but she contributed to American literature and to abolition in ways that still impact us today.

Being a liar is usually wrong, but in Mattie's case, we might find it in our hearts to forgive her. •

THE LIAR:

WILLIAM HENRY IRELAND

DATE: 1796

THE LIE: That he found a lost play by William Shakespeare

REASON: To make his dad love him

Trying to make your parents proud is not unusual, but some people will go a long way to do it. **William Henry Ireland** wanted his father's approval so badly that he pretended to find lost Shakespearean documents (and a supposedly lost play) just to make his dad happy.

William's father, Samuel Ireland, was the ultimate Shakespeare fanboy. Samuel was an artist who wrote and illustrated travel books. He adored books and made a hobby of collecting them. He was particularly fond of Shakespeare. (Keep in mind that Shakespeare died in 1616, more than 100 years before Samuel was born.) Samuel was such a Shakespeare aficionado that he read his favorite Bill Shakespeare plays and sonnets to the whole family each night after dinner.

Samuel was always trying to expand his collection of Shakespeare memorabilia. When William was young, Samuel took him on a trip to Stratford, the town where Shakespeare was born. Samuel was delighted to purchase a chair and a coin purse that allegedly belonged to the great playwright. (Pro tip: Always verify artifacts. Samuel's purchases were probably fakes.)

The shopping experience gave William an idea. If Shakespearean collectibles made his dad happy, then all William had to do to be World's Best Son was find some good Shakespeare stuff. Both Samuel and William were keen readers, so a document with Shakespeare's signature seemed like the perfect Father's Day gift. (Not that Father's Day had been invented yet, but you get the idea.)

Obviously, William couldn't just go to eBay or Craigslist. And it wasn't as if Shakespearean documents with authenticated signatures were lying around waiting to be found by William. So William had to do the next best thing: create a forgery.

THIRTEEN WILLIAM SHAKESPEARE FACTS

1. He was born and died on the same day — April 23. (Different years, of course.)
2. He had seven siblings: Joan, Margaret, Gilbert, Joan II, Anne, Richard, and Edmund.
3. He had eight children with his wife, Anne Hathaway.
4. He was eighteen when he got married. Anne was twenty-six. She was an original cougar.
5. Their first child was born six months after William and Anne's marriage. You do the math there.
6. He had twins named Hamnet and Judith. Poor Hamnet died at age eleven.
7. He was Catholic.
8. He was friends with Queen Elizabeth I.
9. He had an earring in one ear. (Lots of fashionable men had an earring at this time. It was a pirate custom. Pirates allegedly wore one gold earring to cover funeral expenses.)
10. His parents, wife, and kids were probably all illiterate.
11. He frequently performed in his own plays.
12. He invented or popularized almost 2,000 words in the English language. One of those words was *assassination*.
13. He invented a number of girls' names that are still popular today: Miranda, Olivia, Jessica, and Cordelia.

You might think producing a forged document is easy, but it's much harder than it appears. William had to teach himself how to make an ink that would appear to be from the sixteenth century. Getting hold of authentic period paper was less of a problem. William came up with the brilliant solution of removing blank pages of parchment documents from his workplace. (He was an apprentice to a lawyer, so he had access to deeds and other legal papers that were very old.) All William had to do was add a William Shakespeare signature — using his special ink — to an old existing document. And that was exactly what he presented to his father as a gift in 1794.

Samuel was delighted. He had the document authenticated by an expert. The "expert" said, "Yup, it checks out. Everything looks good here."

William was probably very relieved, and for once, he had his father's approval. Imagine how good he felt!

Not completely stupid, Samuel did ask where William obtained such an amazing treasure. William told a lie so thin here that you have to wonder if Samuel might have been a little simple. William told his father that he found the document in a friend's mansion. This is the historical equivalent of telling your parents that you missed curfew because the clock on your phone broke.

Samuel was gloriously gullible. He was so happy with his clever son that he asked if William could get any more of Shakespeare's writing from his mysterious friend with the mansion. William had to go back to work with his ink and his old parchments from his workplace. The more William produced, the happier Samuel was. For the first time, William felt like his father was proud of him.

Over time, William got creative with his fakes. He gave his father fake love letters written to Anne Hathaway, Shakespeare's wife (not the actress from *The Princess Diaries*). He gave his father books with marginalia that he claimed Shakespeare wrote. William himself wrote it. (Marginalia, by the way, refers to the small notes and underlining that readers make in the books they own.)

William was pretty psyched about how happy his father was. If he had stopped with the documents and marginalia, he probably never would have been found out. His father would have died a happy man. But William got greedy.

In 1796 William presented to his father a "lost" Shakespearean play called *Vortigern and Rowena*. (The plot is tough to outline, but all you need to know is that it has lots of power-hungry people, mistaken identities, and young lovers who can't be together.) Of course William (Ireland, not Shakespeare) had written the play himself. Surprisingly, Samuel's team of "experts" was convinced it was real. And that's when things started to go south for William.

People were so excited about this found Shakespearean play that they decided to stage it at Drury Lane Theatre in London. The play's lead actor was a well-known and respectable theater star by the name of John Philip Kemble. John knew the play wasn't very good, but, like many others, he believed that was because Shakespeare must have written it when he was young. Little did he know that William Ireland wrote it, and William stunk at writing.

Meanwhile, Samuel was so excited about his new memorabilia pieces that he started showing them to anyone who wanted to admire his treasures. Suddenly, it wasn't just Samuel's friends authenticating the documents. Now, scholars, historians, and experts from all over the place were examining Samuel's supposedly historical documents in good light and with ample time to spot any mistakes or inconsistencies.

DETECTING FORGERY

Forgery detectives have a tough job. In order to detect art forgery, experts have to do two kinds of analysis: stylistic and technical.

Stylistic analysis involves examining brushstrokes, iconography, documentation, and the wear of an object. (If a canvas is very old, it should show signs of wear and tear in certain places.)

Technical analysis is more scientific. It involves the use of ultraviolet rays to examine canvas and pigment. It can include X-rays and chemical analysis. Some objects can even be carbon-dated.

Before technical analysis techniques were possible, experts had to rely mostly on documentation, which could be forged by people who had a few key skills.

While the whole world was discussing whether or not these documents were real, the Drury Lane Theatre was moving full steam ahead with the performance. Bad play or not, opening night tickets were going like hotcakes. The play might have gone off without a hitch — with people pretending it wasn't bad in order to avoid looking stupid or uncultured — but a Shakespearean scholar named Edmond Malone ruined everything.

Just two days before the play opened, Edmond released a book that attacked all the documents Samuel claimed to have. Edmond was no dummy, and he questioned how it was possible for William to happen upon these priceless historical documents in an anonymous friend's mansion. Suddenly, all eyes were on William and his big fat lies.

The play did go on — to a packed house — but it was awful. It ran for just the one night. After that, too many people had read or heard about Edmond's book. With so many people closely examining the supposed Shakespearean artifacts, it wasn't long before William was forced to admit he'd been lying all along. He confessed because people believed it was his father who had done the forgeries, and he didn't want his father to be blamed. William's last gift to his father was admitting his lies, though not everyone believed William's confession.

In 1805 William published his full confession in a book he called *The Confessions of William Henry Ireland*. Unfortunately, William's apology was not very sincere. The reality was that he wanted a literary career and he wanted his father to love him. The only thing he was sorry about was that he got caught. On top of that, many people still believed that Samuel was the mastermind behind the whole plan. William was known for being a little bit on the dumb side, so people didn't believe he had the capability to pull off relatively convincing fakes.

Samuel died with his reputation in tatters because of William's lies. As for William, he had to move to France where nobody knew him. He died in 1835, having never become a literary star. Even now, the only thing he is remembered for is his ill-conceived Shakespearean forgeries.

If he wanted his father's love, he would have been better off sending him a Hallmark card. Or maybe just a nice tie. •

FRANK ABAGNALE

DATE: 1964–1969

THE LIE: That he was a pilot, a surgeon, a lawyer, and a professor

REASON: To make cashing bad checks easier

Frank Abagnale was just a normal kid, born in 1948 in New York to Frank and Paulette Abagnale. Frank might have grown up to be an ordinary person, but his life took a weird series of turns. Because of those turns, he grew up to be one of the world's most successful liars, at least for a short time.

Frank's mom left the family when he was young. He lived with Frank Sr., who managed a stationery business. Frank Sr. would take Frank Jr. to business meetings where Frank Jr. learned all about the paper business. That not-very-exciting knowledge would become critical to his later success as a criminal.

In Frank's spare time as a kid, he took up shoplifting. Eventually he got caught. After that, he figured out how to run a scam using his father's gas card. It worked like this: Frank would go to a filling station and buy, say, five dollars of gas. He would then have the clerk charge him twenty dollars. Frank would give the clerk a few bucks and pocket the rest. That scam worked until his father caught him and sent him to reform school.

Frank hated his new school and ran away at the age of sixteen. He found it difficult to get a good-paying job at such a young age, so he got creative. Taking what he learned about printing from his father's stationery shop, he created a fake ID. The new ID showed him to be twenty-six years old. It was definitely easier to get jobs as a twenty-six-year-old, but without a college degree and experience, he could only get entry-level jobs, which didn't pay much.

It was time for a new scam. Frank decided to cash bad checks. Before long, banks were getting suspicious of him. After all, there are only so many banks to scam in any given geographic area. One day, while waiting in line at a bank and hoping for a teller who didn't know him, Frank noticed that airline pilots in uniform had a much easier time convincing bank tellers to cash checks. So Frank called up Pan American Airlines and told them he was a pilot who lost his uniform while traveling. Pan Am assumed it was just a case of lost luggage, a common occurrence, so they told him to come down to the office and get a new uniform. He used a fake pilot ID and picked up a uniform (he also charged the cost of it to some other pilot). With his new duds, he could go into a bank anywhere he wanted and use his uniform as proof that he was a credible person, the sort of person who wasn't writing bad checks.

Convincingly playing a pilot at a bank was pretty easy, so Frank figured he would take the next step. He started dating Pan Am stewardesses. Then he could ask all kinds of questions about a pilot's job. He once even pretended to be doing research for a paper he was writing about airline pilots. People love to be helpful, so Pan Am employees told him tons of information.

Frank was a smart guy (even at sixteen years old), and it didn't take long before he knew how to pretend convincingly to be a pilot. He forged an FAA license, and with that he was able to fly whenever he wanted. Over the course of five years, Frank flew to twenty-six countries and racked up about a million miles. All the while he was traveling, he was cashing bad checks and making a whole lot of money.

Flying around must have gotten a little boring because Frank decided to move to Atlanta where he pretended to be a doctor. That's right. He went from pretending to be a pilot to pretending to be a doctor. Once again, he hung around in hospitals and figured out how to *sound* like a pediatric doctor. He was good enough at the job that he was even promoted. He liked being a doctor well enough, until disaster struck when one of his misdiagnoses almost cost a child's life. Frank left the hospital quickly and quietly.

It was time for a new career. In Louisiana, Frank forged test results indicating that he had passed the bar. Then he was a lawyer. When people started getting suspicious, he picked up and moved again. In Utah, he pretended to be a sociology professor and taught at Brigham Young University.

PRISON LIFE

Frank spent time at the Perpignan prison in France. The prison was well known for its horrible treatment of inmates. His cell was nothing more than a stone floor, and he was forced to live in his own urine and excrement. He almost died of starvation. It's a good thing for him that he was sent to a nicer prison in Sweden after just six months.

In another city, he was a film director. By the end of five years, he had used eight different identities and had more careers than anyone could possibly have in one lifetime.

Frank might have continued his life of crime, but at the age of twenty-one, he was caught by police in France. An ex-girlfriend — a Pan Am stewardess, naturally — saw a "Wanted" poster of him and turned him in. Frank went to prison for six months in France. He then spent another six months in jail in Sweden. Finally, he came back to the United States to serve a twelve-year prison sentence for stealing more than $2,000,000.

After Frank had served five years, the FBI decided he would be an excellent asset for detecting and preventing fraud. After all, Frank had proven himself to be a bit of a genius. The FBI paroled him when he was twenty-six with the requirement that he work with law enforcement to prevent crime.

Preventing crime is exactly what Frank has done for more than forty years. He even works on preventing cybercrime now. He says it's "4,000 times easier today to con people" because of all the information we have at our fingertips online and the ease in which we can design and print forgeries.

THE HOLLYWOOD TREATMENT

You may have heard of Frank before. His life story was the subject of Steven Spielberg's 2002 movie *Catch Me if You Can,* starring Tom Hanks and Leonardo DiCaprio. The movie was based on Frank's 1980 memoir of the same title.

The real Frank was concerned about Leonardo playing him because he worried Leonardo wouldn't portray him as suave enough, but he didn't need to worry: Leonardo is pretty suave. Frank has a cameo in the movie. He arrests Leonardo in France, the site of the real Frank's arrest.

In the movie, Frank's father is played by Christopher Walken. In real life, Frank never saw his father again after he left home at the age of sixteen.

If you loved the movie, you might love the Broadway musical that opened in 2011 and later went on tour until 2013. Keep your eyes open for more performances.

Frank's work with the FBI has been important in spotting possible scams before they happen. For example, when a company presented a new model of a cash machine with a small, plastic window where cash comes out, Frank immediately saw a problem. He demonstrated an easy scam: He glued the window shut, and then waited for people to get cash. Each time the person was unable to open the glass door, the person simply left. Once money was in the window, Frank could break the plastic and steal the money. That cash machine model was axed. Cash machines now have slots rather than windows.

No longer a criminal, Frank is happy to live in a country that allows for redemption. He reminds people that he committed his crimes when he was young and stupid (not that that's an excuse). But since then, he's paid back the millions of dollars he stole and has tried to set a good example for his children, one of whom grew up and graduated from the FBI Academy.

He lives in Charleston, South Carolina, with his wife of almost forty years. Frank's company, Abagnale & Associates, continues to advise companies and individuals all over the world on security issues.

Frank proves that the best way to prevent crime is to ask a former expert criminal. •

MILLI VANILLI

DATE: 1990
THE LIE: That Rob and Fabrice were singing
REASON: To sell records

In the late 1980s, a German music producer named Frank Farian assembled a group of musicians who produced some really great music. Frank knew their songs were guaranteed hits. The only problem was the musicians were middle-aged and not all that interesting to look at, a big problem in the golden age of music videos. So Frank hired two gorgeous models to dance and lip-synch the tunes. And that's how the award-winning musical group **Milli Vanilli** was born.

The models were two men named **Rob Pilatus** and **Fabrice (Fab) Morvan**. Rob and Fab were young professional dancers with long, black dreadlocks and piercing dark eyes. They were beautiful, the perfect pair to put on album covers, feature in music videos, and present at fan events, including live shows.

Rob and Fab were not singers, but Frank didn't think that mattered. He reasoned that a lot of musical groups before Milli Vanilli used lip-synching in video and live performances. What was the harm, he reasoned, in giving us a couple of male models to look at while we listened to catchy songs?

Keep in mind that nobody knew Rob and Fab weren't singing. Lip-synching may have been common in the music biz (and still is), but people assumed that the singers they were seeing on stage had simply recorded the songs in studio. Rob and Fab, though, never set foot in the studio. They weren't even back-up singers on their own music!

Milli Vanilli became a worldwide success. Their most famous songs were "Blame It on the Rain," "Baby Don't Forget My Number," and "Girl I'm Gonna Miss You." All three were number one singles in the United States and in other countries. One album went platinum. Another one went gold. Milli Vanilli sold thirty million singles, an incredible number even now.

The videos are still available online and are hilarious artifacts of the late 1980s. In the video for "Baby Don't Forget My Number," Rob and Fab perform a strange little dance while wearing spandex leggings, jackets with shoulder pads, and weird hats and headbands.

It seemed like everyone loved Milli Vanilli. In 1990 they even won a Grammy. They were taking the music world by storm, impressing fans and critics. Their songs were in constant rotation on every Top 40 radio station, and MTV played their videos all the time. They were poised to be long-term stars, like Madonna or Michael Jackson. But something happened that changed everything.

Rob had a drug problem and was reportedly getting increasingly difficult to work with. He told Frank, the producer, that he wanted to sing. Frank knew that would be a problem because Rob was not a professional singer, so he told Rob no. Rob got angry and threatened to blow the whistle on the lie. But Rob played his trump card too soon. Frank was so fed up with Rob's behavior that he exposed the lie himself. Frank told the whole world that Rob and Fab were fakes.

Everyone was shocked. Milli Vanilli was stripped of their Grammy just months after winning it. Arista Records not only dropped the group, but took the record out of circulation altogether. (You can find Milli Vanilli cassettes now, but only if you look at yard sales or thrift stores.)

Frank was the one who came up with the lie in the first place, but he wasn't punished nearly as much as Rob and Fab. Fans felt betrayed, and since they'd never seen Frank — producers aren't exactly public faces — they directed all their anger at Rob and Fab. The two talented dancers became laughingstocks, deeply hated by the fans who had loved them just days before.

Part of the reason fans and music industry people were so angry was the time period. Pop music of the late '80s and early '90s was constantly criticized for being fake or phony. Fans were questioning performers who looked like studio creations but who didn't have much talent. (The Grunge movement in the '90s was at least partially a response to the slick and packaged look and feel of '80s pop music.) To fans, the Milli Vanilli scam seemed like more evidence that pop music was nothing more than a big joke.

Rob and Fab tried to redeem themselves by releasing their own album in 1993. Fans weren't even a little bit interested. The album only sold 2,000 copies, and you have to figure that at least ten of those copies were bought by their mothers!

The pressure and the public excoriation didn't help Rob's drug problem. He got worse and worse until eventually he died in 1998 of an overdose. He was only thirty-three years old. Fab fared a little better. He's still around working as a dancer and trying to overcome his reputation as a pretender.

Frank, the producer, had a much easier time. He went on to produce other groups, including La' Bouche and Le Click. They might not have been powerhouses like Milli Vanilli, but Frank certainly managed to continue his career in music, something Rob and Fab found impossible to do.

MILLI VANILLI FAN CLUB

If you are a Milli Vanilli super-fan, you are in luck. There's a Facebook fan club page just for you. The short description says this: "When music was music, and now Maroon 5?"

Take that, Maroon 5.

CHANGE TO EIGHT FAMOUS SINGERS WHO HAVE BEEN ACCUSED OF LIP-SYNCHING

1. Mariah Carey on *Good Morning America* in 2008
2. Britney Spears at the Video Music Awards in 2007
3. Ashlee Simpson on *Saturday Night Live* in 2004
4. Beyoncé at the presidential inauguration in 2013
5. Michael Jackson at Motown's 25th anniversary in 1983
6. Luciano Pavarotti at the Olympics in 2006
7. 50 Cent at the BET Awards in 2007
8. Madonna at the Super Bowl in 2012

In later interviews, Fab points out that he and Rob were just two players in a very carefully orchestrated lie, yet the public and the music industry blamed the two of them for everything. In reality, they were victims themselves. They were young and eager to be stars. A big-time music producer offered them a chance to be famous, and they took it. It doesn't make their lie right, but it does suggest that Rob and Fab deserve at least a little sympathy.

Fab astutely points out that today music producers use Auto-Tune on singers all the time. He wonders if that's just another form of pretending. It's a good question to ponder, but the real difference between Milli Vanilli and singers who lip-synch in performance or use Auto-Tune is in the degree of pretending. Milli Vanilli was created with the express intent of never letting Rob or Fab open their mouths unless someone else's voice was streaming through the speakers.

Auto-Tune and lip-synched concerts are generally acceptable to music fans, which shows that we don't mind a little deception. But Frank pushed music lying to a level that not even Milli Vanilli's biggest fan (this gal right here) could accept. •

JAMES FREY

DATE: 2003
THE LIE: That he was a criminal who spent time in jail
REASON: To sell books

Unless you live under a rock, you know that the great-and-mighty media mogul Oprah had a book club. And if you were an author and your book got picked by Queen Oprah, your life changed forever. Your book would be a best seller and you would probably be a household name.

Imagine how excited **James Frey** was when Oprah selected his memoir, *A Million Little Pieces*, for her book club in 2005. The book sold more than three million copies and was translated into twenty-eight languages. Oprah talked effusively about how much she loved it, which is probably the biggest compliment any author can ever receive.

James might have gone on to write more memoirs except for one thing: His memoir wasn't completely true.

Here are some of the things he said in his book that were exaggerated or partially untrue

- He was arrested fourteen times.
- He was wanted by the police in three states.
- He assaulted police officers in Ohio.
- He spent three months in jail.
- He might have killed a person.
- He was part of a tragic train accident that killed two girls.
- He had two root canals without painkillers.

It turns out that James was not telling the stories exactly as they happened. True, he was a drug addict (he started drinking and doing drugs when he was fourteen), but some clever researchers discovered that he was not quite the person he pretended to be. He only spent five hours in custody at a police station. He ended up with traffic tickets, not jail time. He was not involved in an assault on police officers, and there is absolutely no evidence that he had anything to do with the train accident or that he killed anyone. He admitted that he had no idea whether or not he had dental work without painkillers — even though he described the event in great detail in his book.

When the truth came out, readers were angry. Some wanted James to "burn in hell." That's pretty angry. But I bet nobody was as mad as Oprah, who felt like she and her fans had been "betrayed" and "duped." She maintained her reputation had been damaged by recommending a memoir that purported to be truth but was actually poppycock.

Oprah invited James on her show in 2006 to answer her questions, and she wasn't exactly easy on him. James admitted that he took liberties with the truth. His publisher, Nan Talese was just as surprised as anyone, she claimed, that James's stories were not true.

At one point, James did reveal that he initially pitched the book as a novel; in fact, it was apparently rejected by multiple publishers when it was submitted as a novel. James's book was only interesting to the publishing world, apparently, when it was described as a memoir and therefore wholly true.

His former agent, Kassie Evashevski, always called his work a memoir and she had no idea that it was largely fictional. The real story of who knew what will probably never surface because James signed a nondisclo-

Before the Oprah debacle, James wrote a screenplay. The screenplay was made into a movie in 1998. It was called *Kissing a Fool*, and it starred David Schwimmer. You might know him best as Ross from *Friends*.

sure agreement, which means that he can't talk about certain things or else he can be subject to legal action.

The publisher offered refunds to any readers who had purchased James's book, believing it was true. Most people didn't submit their book for a refund, which seems to suggest that many readers didn't care if the book was true or false. Oprah, however, stood by her argument that James damaged her credibility by passing off his story as true.

The scandal surrounding James's fictional memoir did raise interesting questions about how true a memoir has to be. Other famous memoir writers, like Augusten Burroughs and David Sedaris, have been questioned about altering details in their stories. Like every good writer, they know that a life story is pretty boring if you tell it exactly how it happened.

On other hand, it's not fair to readers to just make up a bunch of stuff and pass it off as true. Readers and writers of memoirs today often talk about how much tweaking an author can do before a memoir turns into a novel. It's a fine line, one that James crossed, according to many readers.

James's credibility was certainly strained because of his lies, but surprisingly, he is still a writer. He wrote a young adult book (published in October of 2014) called *Endgame*. It's about a planet similar to Earth where twelve races exist. Young people must fight to the death to save bloodlines. If you think that sounds a lot like *The Hunger Games*, you are right. Fans of Suzanne Collins's *The Hunger Games* were livid that James's novel is so similar to an iconic young adult series. Nevertheless, James's publisher paid him a $2,000,000 advance for the novel.

James's story seems to suggest that pretenders can be forgiven — and get rich! •

LONELYGIRL15

DATE: June 2006–September 2006
THE LIE: That Lonelygirl15 was a real girl vlogging from her bedroom
REASON: To make a compelling show people wanted to watch

In 2006 YouTube watchers were obsessed with a vlogger (video blogger) named Lonelygirl15 (known as LG15). LG15 was supposedly a sixteen-year-old homeschooled girl named Bree Avery who lived with her ultra-religious parents. She had an adorable video editor named Daniel, who had a mega-crush on her. Her strict parents were trying to keep the two lovebirds apart. Through a series of two-minute vlogs, Bree told the world her story — sometimes while wearing a pink feather boa and talking to a purple monkey puppet.

Her vlogs are still online, and if you watch them, you'll see that Bree seems like a regular teenager. She has long, straight brown hair and perfectly shaped eyebrows. Her dark eyes are beautiful and expressive. She wears jeans and simple tanks or tees. Her bedspread is pink and covered with stuffed animals. Sometimes she looks awkward, especially when she doesn't know what to say, but she always makes you feel like she's talking directly to you. And her videos are so confessional that you get the feeling you are watching a kind of teen soap opera in diary form.

YouTube subscribers love Bree. Since she debuted in 2006, she has had well over two million views. At the height of her fame, she was getting 125,000 views a day. For many weeks, hers was the most subscribed channel on YouTube.

In September of 2006, the truth came out: Bree wasn't a teenager. She was a twenty-something actress named Jessica Rose, and she was a graduate of the New York Film Academy. Jessica was hired by a guy named **Mesh Flinders** (yup, that's really his name) to play Bree. Mesh wanted to introduce the world to a new kind of TV show: the Web series. So he came up with the LG15 concept.

You might think people stopped watching once they realized Bree wasn't a real teen, but you'd be wrong. The show's numbers actually went up, even after the world knew it was a scripted show. Mesh went on to tell Bree's story for two more years.

Before LG15, Mesh was just a normal guy who happened to live with his grandmother. When he moved out and got his own apartment in Beverly Hills, he figured he could use his bedroom to shoot videos. He really wanted to get into the film business and had unsuccessfully tried to sell his scripts. He and his business partners — Greg Goodfried, a lawyer, and Miles Beckett, a med school dropout — decided to create a Web series about a teen girl who was fighting with her overprotective parents. They hired Jessica to play the part of Bree.

Mesh and his partners decided that Bree would be more interesting if viewers thought she was real. Greg, Mesh's lawyer friend, said they couldn't get into any legal trouble if they were careful never to lie publicly. If asked whether LG15 was real, Mesh and Jessica were instructed to evade the question. Legally, they couldn't be accused of lying.

By the way, don't try this legal argument on your parents. It never works. Let me show you what will happen.

> **Parents:** Did you back the car into a fire hydrant and flood the entire neighborhood?
> **You:** Gosh, the person who did that must have been a horrible driver.
> **Parents:** So it wasn't you?
> **You:** Look! I think I see the Flenkersons' poodle floating away!

See what I mean? Not technically lying, but you are evading the question and thereby lying by omission. Mesh and his buddies were exploiting a legal technicality.

For weeks, people believed Bree was real, but Jessica needed to get a second job to make ends meet. (Even though she was on a hit YouTube show, she wasn't making any money.) She was set to start working as a server at TGI Fridays, but Mesh was scared someone would recognize her and spoil the show. So Mesh found an investor (his business partner's dad) and starting paying Jessica $500 a week. All she had to do was shoot a few two-minute videos. Oh, and she had to stay inside as much as possible and wear sunglasses if she absolutely had to go out. Mesh was pretty committed to this thing.

After a few months, people started to get suspicious of LG15. For one thing, the high-quality video and editing seemed pretty advanced. Mesh

addressed that issue by having Bree say her super-smart boyfriend Daniel was doing it, but viewers questioned whether a teenager had that kind of skill. Other viewers noticed that Bree's story arc felt too much like a script. Rarely does life happen as tidily and orderly as Bree's life seemed to.

The final nail in the coffin appeared when armchair sleuths discovered that LG15's domain was registered just a month before her first vlog, which threw red flags all over the place. There was an abundance of evidence that cast suspicion on Bree.

Online discussions about whether or not Bree was real got really deep. One person searched online for every item Bree had in her room and discovered everything came from Target. (By the way, when Mesh first started the series, he would film and then change the bedspread and the pictures back to his own stuff when he was done shooting. He got tired of that and just started sleeping in the room with all of Bree's things after the filming was complete for the day.) Other posters scoured the Internet looking for any evidence that might prove once and for all if Bree was real.

Real journalists wrote stories about whether LG15 was real or not. Stories ran in *Business Week*, the *Los Angeles Times*, and the *New York Times*. They didn't break the story, though. That honor went to eighteen-year-old Matt Foremski, whose dad was a blogger for the *Silicon Valley Watcher*. It

INTERNET HISTORY QUIZ

See how well you score on the following quiz. Answers are below.

1. **What year was the first website launched?**
   a. 1995
   b. 1975
   c. 1984
   d. 1990

2. **What was the first webcam (at Cambridge University) used for?**
   a. Taking pictures of someone's butt
   b. Saying "Hi Mom!"
   c. Putting on a show with finger puppets
   d. Watching the coffee pot to see when coffee was fresh brewed

3. **What was the name of the first search engine?**
   a. W3 Catalog
   b. Wizard Search
   c. Bob's Search Engine
   d. C-3PO

was Matt who found a MySpace page for Jessica Rose. The page had been deleted, but the photos were still available. Those photos revealed that Jessica was an actress. She was not Bree, a teen girl who loved science and turned techy boys into mush with her winning smile and smart monologues.

Mesh and his collaborators were forced to reveal themselves and admit that Jessica was just pretending to be Bree, a wholly made-up character. Mesh admitted that his original plan was to use Bree's videos as a teaser for a DVD movie. He was surprised when LG15 caught on, and so he ran with it. Even after the hoax was revealed, Mesh and his friends continued to make LG15 videos that many people watched. (In later installments, Bree toys with the idea of joining a cult. It gets pretty crazy.)

Mesh might have been guilty of lying, but he did do something that changed our culture: He showed that the Internet could tell stories in ways we'd never thought of before. He demonstrated that a Web show is not

4. **The first pizza ordered online was from Pizza Hut in 1994. What kind of pizza was it?**
    a. Anchovies and green peppers
    b. Pepperoni and mushroom
    c. Double cheese
    d. Sausage-stuffed crust

5. **What was the first item to sell on eBay? (Hint: It sold for $4,000 in 1995.)**
    a. A Nirvana concert tee
    b. A poster of a hamster snuggling with a kitty
    c. A signed pair of Marky Mark's underwear
    d. A grilled cheese sandwich

6. **What was the first video to go viral via email?**
    a. A dancing baby
    b. A sneezing dog
    c. A crying elephant
    d. A farting goat

ANSWERS:

1.d 2.d 3.a 4.b 5.c 6.a

like a TV show or a movie. It's something altogether different that can be compelling and emotionally riveting.

LG15 seemed on the verge of changing entertainment forever, but it didn't. Unfortunately for Mesh, his production didn't usher in fame, fortune, or a movie deal. Mesh Flinders is still not a household name (though it should be — I stand behind my original assessment that it's a hilarious name).

But what Mesh did do was open the YouTube doors to many other vloggers. And he showed us you don't need an expensive camera or editing equipment to tell good stories.

That seems like a pretty big accomplishment for a dude who lived with his grandma until he was twenty-seven years old. Well done, Mesh. •

CHAPTER 6:
INHERITANCE SEEKERS

THE LIAR:

CASSIE CHADWICK

DATE: 1879–1905

THE LIE: That she was an heiress and descendent of a very rich and famous man

REASON: To make it easier to bilk banks

Cassie Chadwick would not have stood out in a crowd. She had mousy brown hair, a round face with no discernible chin, and a smug, thin-lipped smile. She looked a tiny bit like Mrs. Oleson from that old TV show *Little House on the Prairie*. She was just a plain girl from Ontario, Canada, but she was also a criminal mastermind.

Cassie Chadwick's real name was **Elizabeth "Betty" Bigley**. She was born in 1857 to a railroad worker and a housewife who must have liked each other an awful lot because they had eight kids in total. Betty lost most of her hearing when she was quite young, which caused her to have a speech impediment. She was probably self-conscious about her speech, so she didn't talk much. She sure spent a lot of time cooking up schemes, though.

When she was just thirteen, she masterminded her first swindle. She went to a bank and told a clerk that her uncle died and left her an inheritance. She was so convincing that the bank gave her an advance check upon her word that the inheritance was on its way. She was eventually caught, but her punishment was pretty mild: They simply told her not to do it again. (Imagine the bank manager patiently telling her, "Now, Betty, please don't rob the bank again.")

Betty waited until she was twenty-two to try her next scam. She saved up some money and bought expensive letterhead. Then she sent herself a letter from a fake attorney. The letter said that she been left $15,000 by a rich philanthropist who had just kicked the bucket. With the letter in hand, she went to shops all over town and wrote checks over the amount of the items she was buying. Shop owners trusted she was good for it; after all, the letter "proved" that she had thousands of dollars coming. She even created fake calling cards stating that she was an heiress. People were impressed enough that they didn't question her.

She did eventually get caught, but she didn't go to jail. She was released on grounds of insanity (which seems like a reason *not* to release her). She figured she better get out of town, so she headed to Cleveland, Ohio, to live with her sister Alice.

Betty behaved herself for a short time until she came up with the idea of taking out a bank loan. She used everything in Alice's house — including the furniture and the wall hangings — as collateral. Alice's husband was so mad when he found out (understandably) that he immediately kicked her out of the house.

Alone with no money, Betty needed a place to live and a means of survival. So she got married. The lucky groom was a doctor named Wallace Springsteen. They were happy for about eleven days. Then Wallace found out about all the scams she had pulled in her past. He divorced her on the twelfth day of their marriage. (That makes Kim Kardashian's first marriage seem like a lifetime.)

With no husband, Betty decided she needed to get a job. She opened up a fortune-telling business under the name Mademoiselle Marie Rosa. She claimed to be a descendant of famous people, including General William Tecumseh Sherman. The fortune business did well enough, but she wanted even more money. She supplemented her income by marrying a man who had the good sense to die a few years after they married. He left Betty $50,000. They had a son named Emil, but Betty sent him to Canada to live with her parents.

When people in Cleveland got suspicious of her, she moved to Toledo and became Mademoiselle Lydia DeVere. She was just mysterious enough to attract the attention of Joseph Lamb, who was a simple man (to put it nicely). He married her as quickly as he could get her to the altar.

While married, she wrote bad checks all over town. (One wonders what happened to the $50,000 she had from her previous husband.) When she got caught, the police assumed Joseph was in on it. He went to jail with her even though he had no idea what she was up to. Fortunately, the police sorted it out and released Joseph.

Betty spent three and a half years in jail. Joseph divorced her, so she was all alone and penniless. You might have assumed that she spent those years repenting and vowing to live on the straight and narrow. You would be wrong. Betty's biggest scam was still to come.

She got out of jail, moved back to Cleveland, and promptly changed her name to Cassie. She soon married a wealthy doctor named Leroy Chadwick. Cassie told Leroy she was an etiquette instructor for young ladies, so he assumed she was a woman of upstanding moral character. (Clearly, there was no shortage of stupid men in Ohio.)

Leroy did have money, but not as much money as Cassie spent. Their house was filled with beautiful and expensive pieces, including a chair that played music when someone sat in it. (Why anyone would want such a thing is open for debate.) She even had a gold organ in her sitting room. (By organ, I mean the musical instrument, not a golden liver or something, though I wouldn't put such a thing past Cassie.)

Leroy's money wasn't going to last forever, so Cassie came up with a brilliant and complicated scheme. In 1902 she left Cleveland on a train for New York City. From there, she took a carriage to a fancy hotel called the Holland House. She knew her husband's friend, James Dillon, would be there. James was a lawyer and an incurable gossip. She pretended to run into him in the hotel and feigned great surprised that the two of them would be in New York City at the same time. What a coincidence! After a brief chat, the two decided to share a carriage. Cassie told James she had just one errand to do: She had to stop by her father's house.

Here's where her biggest, boldest, and best scam begins. James was intrigued enough by Cassie's mysterious errands that he agreed to tag along. They chatted inside the carriage while Cassie called out an address to the driver. That address was 2 East 91st Street. James probably recognized it right away. That was the address of the palatial home of Andrew Carnegie, one of the richest men in America. Andrew was an extremely wealthy steel magnate and noted philanthropist. James's jaw probably dropped to the bottom of the carriage.

Upon arrival at Andrew's mansion, Cassie asked James to wait in the carriage while she conducted a quick piece of business with her father. James, probably too surprised to speak, agreed. Cassie went to the door of the house and told either a housekeeper or a butler that she wanted a reference for a maid she was considering hiring. Cassie gave a false name for the maid. Naturally, the staff person was confused and invited Cassie inside as she inquired of other house staff about this maid who claimed to have worked for the Carnegie family. After everyone in the house was thoroughly confused, Cassie told the staff it must have been a mix-up and that she would be on her way. All in all, she spent about thirty minutes inside the house, and as far as James knew, she was speaking to Andrew Carnegie himself. How was James to know that she only spoke to the house staff?

While walking back to the carriage, Cassie theatrically pulled an envelope from her coat pocket, a movement James clearly saw. When she got back into the carriage, he asked her if Andrew was indeed her father. He claims she answered yes. She claims she never officially said one way or the other. Nevertheless, she led James to believe she was Andrew's illegitimate daughter. She swore James to secrecy, and then opened the envelope to reveal promissory notes for large amounts of money. She led James to believe the notes were in exchange for her keeping quiet about her real heritage as the illegitimate daughter of the very famous and rich Andrew Carnegie.

Cassie told James he must never, ever tell anyone her secret, knowing full well that he was loose lipped. Just as she intended, it wasn't long before he had spread the story all over town. On the strength of Andrew's alleged promissory notes, Cassie was able to buy on credit and write bad checks wherever she went. Nobody was going to deny Andrew Carnegie's secret

CARNEGIE LIBRARIES

Andrew loved libraries. That's why he donated $60,000,000 to the creation of more than 1,500 libraries all over America. Andrew believed that libraries would help people help themselves.

Lest you think Andrew was perfect, I should tell you that he could be kind of a jerk. When steel laborers demanded better wages, Andrew told them no because they would simply waste their extra money on junk. Instead, he told them they needed libraries and concert halls to better themselves. You can imagine how that must have frustrated workers who probably needed more money to feed and clothe their children.

ANDREW CARNEGIE'S GOSPEL OF WEALTH

Andrew felt strongly that rich people had a responsibility to give money to the poor; in fact, he thought that the rich should leave almost *all* their money to the poor! In 1889 he wrote an article for a publication called *North American Review* in which he told rich people what their responsibilities were. He wrote that the wealthy must "set an example of modest, unostentatious living, shunning display or extravagance." When they die, they should "provide moderately for the legitimate wants of those dependent upon him." After loved ones are taken care of, the remaining wealth should be used to better communities. According to Andrew, even while rich people are alive, they have an obligation to use their wealth to help others.

How many super-rich people now believe as Andrew did?

love child. Some estimates suggest that she stole about $633,000. That's about $16,500,000 now.

Cassie bilked so many people that she was bound to get caught, and she eventually did. Andrew Carnegie himself was at her trial and was quite unimpressed with the forged promissory notes. He pointed out that they were full of spelling and grammar errors. Still, hundreds of people never questioned them.

In March of 1905, Cassie was sentenced to ten years in prison. Given the amount of money she stole, that seems like a fairly light sentence, but it turned out to be a death sentence. When she was fifty years old, she died in her prison cell. She had only been in prison for a couple of years.

Her memory lives on now, but not in a good way. The only thing she's really remembered for is pretending to have a rich father and then wasting away in prison.

Nobody knows what happened to that gold organ. •

ANNA ANDERSON

DATE: 1920–1984
THE LIE: That she was Anastasia Romanov, a lost Russian princess
REASON: Mental illness, probably

Anastasia Romanov was the youngest daughter of the Russian czar Nicholas II. In 1918, during the Bolshevik Revolution, the czar and his entire family were killed by dissident soldiers. The family was shot in the cellar of the house where they'd been exiled. Their bodies were removed from the house almost immediately. They were burned and then buried. Rumor had it, though, that seventeen-year-old Anastasia escaped and was living somewhere under a false name. A couple of years after the Romanovs were brutally murdered, **Anna Anderson** emerged, claiming to be the lost princess Anastasia. She was not, but she fooled a lot of people for a long time.

Anna was born Franziska Schanzkowska in Poland in 1896. She had dark hair and eyes, full lips, and an intriguing Mona Lisa smile. In 1920 — when she was twenty-four years old — she tried to kill herself by jumping off a bridge in Berlin. She survived. When she emerged from the water, she refused to tell anyone her name. Later, she claimed that she was Anastasia Romanov, but she was too frightened to tell anyone when she was first discovered in the water.

She didn't convince the surviving extended family members of the Romanov clan; they thought she was a fraud from the very beginning. They didn't believe for a second that their beloved Anastasia had escaped the horrific mass murder scene in that dank cellar.

But some very important people thought she was telling the truth. Maria Rasputin, daughter of Grigori Rasputin, a very famous advisor to Nicholas, believed that Anna was really Anastasia. Maria's faith in Anna probably contributed to the story lasting as long as it did. In 1956 there was even a movie made about Anna starring Ingrid Bergman. (Twentieth Century Fox also made an animated movie about Anastasia in 1997. It didn't discuss Anna directly, though.)

Lots of people questioned Anna, and she seemed to have logical answers for everything. She said that she survived the shooting in the cellar because she was wearing clothes with jewels sewed in the lining. The bullet didn't penetrate the stones, she argued. When she wasn't shot, she claimed a soldier then tried to kill her with a bayonet, but the blade was too blunt. She faked death until the soldiers left. Then, Anna argued, she spoke to two brothers who came to remove the bodies. They helped her escape to Romania.

In Romania she changed her name to Anna Anderson, then she went to Berlin. She wanted to come back to Russia, she said, but she was worried her remaining family wouldn't believe her. She was so distraught that she decided to kill herself by jumping off that bridge.

It actually seems like a plausible story. It's true that rumors had circulated that there was at least one missing body in the cellar. And Anna did have scars on her body consistent with bullet and bayonet wounds. She and Anastasia even had a similar foot deformity, which seemed like an awfully big coincidence.

Even when skeptics found reasonable doubt, Anna seemed to have a good explanation. For example, she spoke German, French, and English, but could not speak Russian. She understood it though, and claimed that she was too traumatized by the murder of her family by fellow Russians to speak the language ever again.

People who were closest to Anastasia tested Anna constantly. Some were convinced she knew things that only Anastasia could know. For instance, she referred to animal drawings that had been done for Anastasia. Skeptics argued that some people just wanted to believe Anna was the real deal, and so they were willing to believe anything Anna said. The reality was that she could have learned about the animal drawings any number of ways.

In spite of Anna's very good lies, she was never accepted into the Romanov family. In 1968 she married John Manahan, an American college professor. They moved to Virginia where they became hoarders. They lived in a house full of garbage and a bunch of cats and dogs. Anna died of pneumonia in 1984. She had a round face covered in wrinkles and an expression of sadness, maybe because she was known the world over as a great big fat liar.

In the 1990s the Romanov bodies were exhumed. All the bodies were there, including Anastasia's, and DNA testing proved that Anastasia's body was certainly that of the real Anastasia Romanov.

Anna was cremated after her death, but hair and skin samples (don't ask me where those came from) were tested for DNA. Anna was not a match to the Romanov family. The reality was that she was a Polish factory worker who was mentally ill and who tried to commit suicide all those years ago in Germany. Whether she really believed she was Anastasia or whether she intentionally tried to fool people is unclear.

ANNA ANDERSON IN FILM

Anna's story captivated a lot of people. Two movies have been made about her life. The first one was called *Anastasia*. It premiered in 1956 and starred Ingrid Bergman and Yul Brynner. In the movie, Anna is manipulated by a Russian criminal into pretending to be Princess Anastasia.

The second movie was called *Anastasia: The Mystery of Anna*. It aired on TV in 1986. The movie starred Amy Irving, the wife of Steven Spielberg. (They later divorced.) The movie also featured Christian Bale in his first role. He played one of the Romanov children.

The Twentieth Century Fox animated movie, called *Anastasia*, came out in 1997, but it doesn't tell exactly Anna's story. Instead, it's about a girl named Anya who is taken advantage of by con men who want her to pretend to be Anastasia in order to make money. The voice of Anya is done by Meg Ryan.

EIGHT FACTS ABOUT RUSSIA

1. The Russian Revolution was actually a series of revolutions that began in 1917.
2. Since 1993, the population of Russia has fallen by more than six million people.
3. Russia is home to 22 percent of the world's trees.
4. Russia has nine time zones. Try getting over jet lag in Russia.
5. The murder rate in America is half that of Russia's.
6. In 1990 Russia traded twenty sea vessels for Pepsi products.
7. Russian bears are addicted to jet fuel. They get high from sniffing the fumes. Don't be surprised if you see a bear on the tarmac. It is looking for its next fix.
8. The average Russian citizen drinks about three pounds of tea a year.

Anna wasn't the first or last person to claim to be Anastasia, but her claim lasted the longest. Perhaps that's because she had the best story and she stuck to it without ever wavering. People today still believe Anna might have been Anastasia, but that's just wishful thinking. DNA is pretty tough to argue.

The reality is that Anastasia's life was tragically cut short by a political revolution. What she might have done with her life if she had survived will forever remain a mystery. And what prompted Anna to tell such a lie is equally unknowable. •

CHAPTER 7:
LADY PIRATES & SOLDIERS

ANNE BONNY & MARY READ

DATE: 1700s

THE LIE: That they were men

REASON: To fight on pirate ships

When you think of pirates, you probably think of men. But some of the fiercest pirates were actually women pretending to be men. **Anne Bonny** and **Mary Read** were two women who fought and plundered alongside men on pirate ships in the eighteenth century. Anne and Mary first appeared in print in a book called *A General History of the Robberies and Murders of the Most Notorious Pirates*. The book was written by a man named Captain Charles Walker in 1724, but Charles was probably Daniel Defoe, an author best known for his novel *Robinson Crusoe*. (The fact that Daniel used a pen name is another case of pretending!)

Anne was born in about 1700 in Cork, Ireland, to a father who was a lawyer and a mother who was his maid. The situation was so scandalous that the family moved to America to get away from the gossip. They landed in what is now Charleston, South Carolina, where her father, William Cormac, began a new law practice. Her mother died of typhoid when Anne was only thirteen.

William had high hopes for his daughter, Anne, but she had a mind of her own. She met a poor sailor named James Bonny and ran off with him when she was only sixteen. William was not pleased; in fact, he disowned Anne.

Not surprisingly, James and Anne had a difficult life. James's job was turning in pirates to the authorities to make money, a dangerous career, as you can imagine. Anne grew bored with him quickly and started having affairs with other men. In 1718 or so, she met a pirate named Captain Jack Rackham. Anne accidentally got pregnant, so Jack took her to Cuba to have the baby. It seems that they probably left the baby there. (Neither of them will be nominated Parent of the Year.)

Rumor has it that Captain Jack paid James to divorce Anne, but James refused to let go of his wife. Nevertheless, Anne didn't go back to James; instead, she joined Jack on a pirate ship. She dressed like a man and fought, swore, and drank with the best of them. (Whether or not the other crewmen knew she was a woman is somewhat unclear. It seems that at least some were aware that she was a woman and Captain Jack's mistress.)

Anne was later captured, as most pirates eventually are. Being a pirate, as you know, is highly illegal. What happened to Anne next is still a mystery. Some evidence suggests that she was released. Given that her father had money and some influence, he may have intervened on her behalf. Other people speculate that she was pregnant. At the time, it was illegal to execute pregnant women. For all we know, Anne went back home to South Carolina and lived a life on the straight and narrow. Or she might have died a lonely death with a ruined reputation.

Daniel Defoe also wrote about Mary Read, another cross-dressing pirate. Mary was born in 1690 or so. Her father was a sea captain who died when she was just a baby. Her mother had very little money, so she dressed Mary as a boy and tried to pass her off to her dead husband's mother as her grandson. Mary's mother knew that old Grandma would give her money for a grandson (but evidently not for a granddaughter).

As it turned out, Mary enjoyed dressing like a boy, so she put on her boy clothes and enlisted as a soldier. While on a ship, Mary met a soldier and took a fancy to him. She casually let him know she was actually a woman. (How she did that, I'll leave to you to imagine.) He was into her once he found out she was a woman. So they got married and settled down to run an inn.

Mary might have been perfectly happy living as a woman for the rest of her life, but her dear husband died unexpectedly, leaving her with no money and lots of debts. Mary did what she did best: She pretended to be a man again and went back to the sea.

BASEBALL PIRATES

Did you know that the professional baseball team the Pittsburgh Pirates was originally called the Alleghenys? The Philadelphia Athletics accused the Alleghenys of stealing — or *pirating* — a player from them. The draft of that player was completely legal, but the name stuck. Beginning in 1891, Pittsburgh's baseball team officially became the Pirates.

She began her pirate career while on a military ship bound for the West Indies. Pirates took over the ship, and instead of defending it, Mary switched sides. The pirates either didn't know or didn't care that she was a woman because they quickly accepted her into their ranks.

While pirating, Mary met Anne. Daniel Defoe, who was somewhat dirty-minded, implies that they might have met when Anne tried to hit on Mary and discovered she was a woman. Some stories of the two women suggest that they went on to be lovers. Others speculate that Daniel might have added that little detail to satisfy his own fantasies.

Daniel's account does suggest that both Mary and Anne were excellent pirates who were better fighters than many men of the day. Daniel writes about a particularly bloody siege on their ship: "None kept the Deck except Mary Read and Anne Bonny, and one more; upon which, she, Mary Read, called those under Deck, to come up and fight like Men, and finding they did not stir, fired her Arms down the Hold amongst them, killing one and wounding others." Anne and Mary clearly had no patience for cowardly men.

Another story suggests that Mary fell in love with a man on her ship. When he was challenged to fight a much bigger and fiercer man, she told

THIRTEEN BEST PIRATE ROMANCE NOVEL TITLES

Romance readers love pirates in their love stories. Here are some of the cheesiest titles. (You'll have to look them up to see their racy pirate covers!)

1. *The Pirate and the Pagan*, by Virgina Henley
2. *Lady Pirate*, by Lynsay Sands
3. *The Captain of All Pleasures*, by Kresley Cole
4. *The Care and Feeding of Pirates*, by Jennifer Ashley
5. *Lady Vixen*, by Shirlee Busbee
6. *Master of Seduction*, by Kinley MacGregor
7. *Velvet Chains*, by Constance O'Banyon
8. *The Pirate and the Puritan*, by Cheryl Howe
9. *Duke by Day, Rogue by Night*, by Katherine Bone
10. *Once Upon a Pirate*, by Nancy Block
11. *Captain Jack's Woman*, by Stephanie Laurens
12. *Seduced by a Pirate*, by Eloisa James
13. *The Pink Pearl*, by Suzette Marquis

her boyfriend that the fight had been rescheduled for a later hour. While the boyfriend slept peacefully below deck, Mary showed up for the fight herself. She won, naturally.

Mary was eventually captured, much like Anne. She, too, was spared from hanging because she allegedly was pregnant. She went to prison and died there of some kind of illness. Unlike Anne, she had no rich father who might have saved her.

Anne and Mary didn't necessarily want to be men, but they wanted to do things women couldn't do at the time. They proved that women could be just as good at criminal acts as any man. They just had to be good liars and even better pretenders. •

DEBORAH SAMPSON

DATE: 1781–1783

THE LIE: That she was a man

REASON: To enlist as a soldier and fight in the Revolutionary War

---

One of the bravest men who fought in the American Revolution wasn't a man at all. It was a woman. **Deborah Sampson** donned a uniform and enlisted. She fought alongside men who forever shaped the history of America.

Drawings of Deborah show her looking very serious and very boyish. Imagine Ted Mosby from *How I Met Your Mother* in Revolutionary War garb. She looks like a woman who could handle a musket. Deborah's difficult early life probably helped her develop the grit she needed to survive one of history's bloodiest wars.

She was born in Massachusetts in 1760. She had six brothers and sisters, which is a lot of mouths requiring a lot of food. When her father vanished at sea, her mother was forced to place the children in other homes in order to survive. (Deborah's father was really not dead as presumed. He simply moved to Maine to get away from his wife and children. Don't worry, karma caught up with him. He died a pauper with no friends or family.)

Deborah went to a couple of different homes where she was expected to do farm work. Her third home was with Deacon Benjamin Thomas, who had ten sons. Deborah worked in the fields with the boys while occasionally attending school in the winter. When she couldn't attend school, she educated herself by looking at the boys' lesson books.

SAM-WHO?

Deborah Sampson's real last name was probably spelled Samson. In 1797 an author named Herman Mann wrote a book about her heroism, but he was such a bad researcher that he spelled her name wrong. His spelling — Sampson — caught on, and to this day Deborah is known by the wrong spelling of her last name.

SEVEN REVOLUTIONARY WAR FACTS

1. The Revolutionary War started because American colonists were forced to pay taxes but were not allowed to represent themselves in Parliament.
2. George Washington was commander of the Continental Army, but he had no previous experience leading an army. Talk about on-the-job training!
3. The first two battles of the war happened in April of 1775. They were in Lexington and Concord, Massachusetts. They were a big win for Washington. He lost eight men. The British lost seventy.
4. The war ended in 1781 in Yorktown, Virginia. George Washington was away from his home for six long years.
5. There were actually two Boston tea parties. The first was the famous one where patriots dumped tea to make a point to the British. One year later, another group of angry colonists staged their own tea party. Both parties cost the British the equivalent of $3,000,000.
6. Most colonists approved of the war, but some didn't. About 20 percent sided with the British.
7. King George knew Britain wasn't going to win the war, but he kept it going to punish the colonists. He wanted to inflict as much harm as possible and hoped to destroy the land altogether. No wonder the colonists didn't like him. He sounds like a real jerk.

When she turned eighteen, Deborah became a schoolteacher. She also toyed with the idea of passing as a man. She even went so far as dressing up like a man, wandering about the village, and seeing if anybody noticed. Fortunately for her, she was tall for a girl. In fact, at five feet seven inches, she was taller than many men. In 1781, when she was confident that she could successfully pass as a man, she enlisted as an infantry(wo)man. As far as we know, she was the first American woman to join a war. She took the name Robert Shurtlief.

She worked hard at concealing that she was a woman. She had to bind her breasts tightly, and she couldn't bathe in the Hudson River with her fellow soldiers. You can imagine that going to the bathroom was probably tough. She must have spent a lot of time hiding behind trees. The other soldiers noticed that "Robert" didn't grow a beard, but they assumed it was because "he" was young. They even gave her the nickname Molly because of her smooth face. Little did they know how close to the truth they were about her real identity.

Some people in her hometown in Massachusetts knew that she was pretending to be a man, but the troops had already begun to march. There was no way to reveal her. Besides, she was already proving her worth as a soldier. "Robert" was known as tough, strong, and patriotic. (That didn't stop her Baptist church from excommunicating Deborah though.)

"Robert" fought in a battle in 1782 and was wounded in the forehead by a sword. The gash left her covered in blood, which hid the more serious wound in her left thigh. That's where she'd been hit by a pistol ball. A doctor bandaged her forehead while she hid her leg injury. Later, she removed the pistol ball herself (with no anesthetic). Her leg never healed properly, but she continued to serve as an American soldier.

In the summer of 1783, "Robert" went to Philadelphia to help control a protest held by soldiers. The war was over, but tensions were still high. When she got there, the city was hit with a massive flu epidemic, and she lost consciousness. This event was her worst nightmare. When she was awake, she could cleverly cover up her female body parts. But while "Robert" was unconscious, Dr. Benjamin Binney of Philadelphia conducted an examination. Deborah's charade was over. Dr. Benjamin sent a letter to General Peterson revealing the true identity of Robert Shurtlief. Shortly after, Deborah was given an honorable discharge from service.

Two years later, a woman again, Deborah met a man named Benjamin Gannet. They married and went on to have three children. Deborah transformed into a farm wife and devoted mother. In 1802 she started doing lectures on a circuit, becoming the first woman in American history to do that. When she spoke publicly, she wore her military uniform.

Deborah eventually received a $4-per-month pension, but it wasn't easy to get at first. Paul Revere asked Congress on her behalf. Congress couldn't argue with the facts: Deborah had served the country with honor, and she deserved the same payment as any man.

POSTHUMOUS AWARDS

Deborah was even more famous after she died. In 1983 the governor of Massachusetts, Michael Dukakis, declared her the official heroine of the state.

When Deborah died in 1827 at the age of sixty-six, her husband applied to receive her pension. Legally, a soldier's wife was entitled to her husband's pension, and Benjamin argued that he ought to get the same treatment. He did. He became the first man in America to get a pension on behalf of female soldier.

Deborah proved that women can be just as brave as men. She just had to lie to prove it. •

CHAPTER 8:
PEN-NAMED WRITERS

BENJAMIN FRANKLIN

DATE: 1722

THE LIE: That he was a middle-aged widow named
   Silence Dogood

REASON: To get published in his older brother's newspaper

Josiah Franklin was father to seventeen children. His tenth child was a son named **Benjamin Franklin**, born in Boston in 1706. He would grow up to be an important historical figure, but before that, he was a secret newspaper columnist.

   Little Ben was an eager student, and unlike his brothers, he had the opportunity to go to school. At that time, the tenth son was considered the "tithe son," which meant that parents were supposed to educate that son for service in the church.

   Ben only went to a school for a short time before Josiah ran low on money. Josiah pulled Ben out and put him to work in the family soap business. Ben hated the soap biz. He much preferred to read books and write. He was so unhappy that he considered running away to sea.

   Josiah caught wind that Ben wanted to run away. He was terrified of losing his beloved son, so he arranged for Ben to work as an apprentice to James Franklin, Ben's older brother. James was a printer, a career that appealed to Ben because he could be around books all day and night. Ben frequently "borrowed" books at night from unsuspecting owners and returned them early in the morning.

   The print shop was not just a makeshift library for Ben — it was also the perfect opportunity for him to work on his writing. He particularly loved writing poetry, but he was a beginner. He studied newspapers to learn how to be a better writer.

   He couldn't read and write all the time, though. He had to earn his keep by working in the print shop, and it wasn't much fun. Ben had to set the type for pamphlets that the shop printed, a time-consuming and tedious job. Then, once the pamphlets were printed, he had to go sell them on the street, an often thankless task that involved standing outside no matter the weather.

Ben's work in the shop contributed toward a certain amount of financial success for his brother James. In 1721 James decided to launch his own newspaper. It was called the *New England Courant*, and it was the third newspaper in the history of Boston. Unlike existing papers, the *New England Courant* had no ties to colonial government, which made it revolutionary in its day.

Ben, who was only fifteen at the time, desperately wanted to write for the paper, but James wouldn't let him. James was a bit of a bully and a little jealous of Ben, who was exceedingly clever. James didn't want Ben to show him up in any way.

When Ben was sixteen, he finally came up with an idea that would allow him to write for James's newspaper without James even knowing. Ben invented an alter ego, a middle-aged woman named Silence Dogood. Ben wrote a letter as Silence and then slipped it under the newspaper office door. In the morning, James found it and shared it with his friends. They loved it. They thought this Silence Dogood was hilarious. You can imagine how

MRS. DOUBTFRANKLIN

BEN'S DAILY SCHEDULE

Ben was a fanatic about scheduling his time. He began every day by asking what good he was going to do that day, and he ended each evening by cataloguing the good he had accomplished. Every hour through the day was accounted for and devoted to improving himself and the world around him.

A typical day for Ben looked like this.

> 5 a.m. to 8 a.m. — Get up, get ready, read, eat breakfast,
> and plan the day
> 8 a.m. to noon — Work
> Noon to 2 p.m. — Read and eat lunch while looking at
> his accounts
> 2 p.m. to 6 p.m. — Work
> 6 p.m. to 9 p.m. — Eat dinner, listen to music, and engage
> in conversation with friends and neighbors
> 9 p.m. to 5 a.m. — Sleep

It's amazing how much someone can get done when he or she doesn't have to check Facebook or Instagram every few minutes!

proud Ben must have felt, but he kept his identity secret and continued to write. At night, he would slip letters written by Silence under the door, and in the morning James would find them and print them. It tickled Ben that James's intelligent friends were so impressed with what he was writing.

All in all, James published at least fourteen Silence Dogood letters in his paper over the course of 1722. "Silence" wrote about all kinds of issues, including freedom of speech, women's rights, and religious hypocrisy. She advised readers to work hard and not drink too much. She referred to herself as "an Enemy to Vice, and a friend to Vertue."

But Silence wasn't all sage advice. She wasn't afraid to mock venerated institutions or ideas other people were scared to question. For example, Silence poked fun at Harvard, saying that the only thing students learned there was how to be conceited. Even James's Harvard-educated friends had a laugh at that because they knew it was at least partially true.

The Silence Dogood letters were a hit with readers. They understood that Silence was a fake name, a common practice at the time, but nobody, including James, suspected Ben was the real writer. Most readers assumed it was a very clever man with an impressive education and impeccable writing credentials.

A minority of readers, however, were literalists. They were convinced that Silence was really a woman, a sage widow dispensing advice on a weekly basis. When Silence announced that she was open to accepting suitors, many men wrote to her volunteering for the job. Imagine how tickled Ben must have been to receive those letters.

At the same time Silence was taking Boston by storm, controversial issues were heating up, and James didn't shy away from addressing them. Debates about smallpox inoculation were sprouting up. Some people thought inoculations were good; other people worried that they would make people sicker. James, never one to avoid a heated debate, even went to jail for a while because of comments he made about the Mather brothers, famous Puritan preachers. Ben had to run the paper for James. Even though he was just a teenager, Ben did an excellent job, maybe even better than James.

If Ben was expecting thanks from James, he must have been sorely disappointed. When James got out of jail, he was as resentful as ever of Ben and continued to treat him poorly. He yelled at him and beat him. Josiah, their father, took Ben's side, which made James even angrier. Ben finally got so fed up that he quit. In 1723 James ran an ad in his own paper: "James Franklin, printer, in Queen's Street, wants a likely lad for an apprentice." That was a pretty big hint that James wanted Ben gone.

Ben left for Philadelphia, where he eventually made a name for himself in science, literature, and politics. He would never write as Silence Dogood again, but he would write under other pen names, including Richard Saunders in *Poor Richard's Almanack*.

In the end, the joke is on James Franklin. Who has ever heard of him? Yet Benjamin Franklin remains a treasured figure of American history. I guess it doesn't pay to be a jerk face. •

THE LIAR:
MARY ANN EVANS

DATE: 1859
THE LIE: That she was a male novelist
REASON: So people would take her more seriously

In a tiny house in a small rural village in England in 1819, a baby girl was born to Robert and Christina Evans. That baby, **Mary Ann Evans**, was the youngest of five children. Mary Ann would grow up to be one of the greatest novelists in all of literary history, but she would be known by her pen name, George Eliot.

Mary Ann grew up in a strict religious and conservative family. She attended boarding school for a few years, but she had to leave school when her mother died. Mary Ann moved home to take care of her father, a land agent. Her father encouraged Mary Ann to continue learning on her own. She was particularly fond of books, so he bought her as many books as he could afford and made sure she had Italian and German lessons. Mary Ann read aloud to her father every night. Their favorite author was Sir Walter Scott.

After years of homeschooling, Mary Ann met an influential couple who would become lifelong friends. Charles and Cara Bray were freethinkers, people who questioned religion. Mary Ann was fascinated by her new friends. They introduced her to important writers and philosophers like Ralph Waldo Emerson, and Mary Ann began to question all the things she'd been taught by her religious father.

Her father was not too happy about the company Mary Ann was keeping. They had their biggest fight when Mary Ann stopped going to church. Like the Brays, she questioned the truth of religion, a big no-no in Mr. Evans's book. He was outraged by her sacrilege, but Mary Ann wouldn't budge. Finally, Mr. Evans offered a compromise: Mary Ann could think and believe whatever she wanted, but she had to go to church and quietly pretend she still believed. That arrangement worked out just for fine for a while.

When Mary Ann was old enough to leave home, she moved to London. She was delighted to have so much freedom. She could think and do as she pleased without interference from her overprotective father. And she didn't have to go to church and pretend to believe anymore.

While in London, she began writing for a publication called the *Westminster Review*, a journal for radicals. She was such an excellent writer that she eventually became an editor of the publication. Bitten by the writing bug, she published a series of stories loosely based on the people she knew in Warwickshire, the village where she was born. Those stories appeared in *Blackwood's Magazine*, a popular publication of the time.

While writing for impressive publications and hanging out with elite intellectuals, Mary Ann met a man named George Henry Lewes. George was considered very ugly, but he was smart and well read. He was a philosopher and actor who had connections to all kinds of interesting people. Mary Ann was smitten. She herself was often described as plain with a very low, unfeminine voice. In drawings, she looks a tiny bit like George Washington with a long nose and a thin face. Images show her brown hair parted serviceably in the middle. George found her beautiful, which is very romantic if you think about it.

The couple seemed perfectly suited to each other. There was only one problem: George was already married. But George and his wife, Agnes, were not your typical married couple of the Victorian era. They believed in free love, which meant that Agnes lived with another man and George was free to pursue other women. That must have suited Mary Ann just fine because she moved in with George. She knew her family wouldn't approve, so she didn't tell them for the first three years that she was with George. But once they found out that she was living in sin with a married man, they were livid.

George and Mary Ann eventually decided that they wanted to spend the rest of their lives together. Divorce wasn't an option for George, so the best he could do was officially separate from Agnes. He and Mary Ann lived together until his death, though they were never able to marry. Still, they were loyal to each other until George died.

While George was alive, their home was a lively one. They had many friends from the literary establishment who frequently showed up to discuss literature, politics, and philosophy. It was an exciting place to be, especially in a Victorian society where radical ideas were considered shocking and immoral.

After the success of her short stories and essays, Mary Ann took up novel writing. Both she and George knew she was a talented writer, but they recognized that she wouldn't be taken seriously as a woman writer. At the time, women writers were associated with romance novels and thus relegated to less serious literature. Mary Ann decided to take on a pen name. A woman writing under a male pseudonym was not uncommon at the time; for one thing, it was much easier to get published if a writer was a man. The Brontë sisters had done the same thing, so Mary Ann was not alone. She picked the name George in honor of her boyfriend. And she decided on Eliot for a last name. She liked the fullness of how the name sounded. Just like that, George Eliot was born.

Mary Ann's first novel, *Adam Bede*, was published in 1859. It was so popular that other writers started taking credit for it. People knew that George Eliot was a pen name, but they couldn't figure out who it was. They assumed it was a man because they didn't believe a woman could write something so smart and erudite.

With a number of good reviews under her belt, Mary Ann finally came forward and admitted she was George Eliot. People were surprised, but they loved the novel so much that most of them didn't care that the author was a woman. But she probably never would have gotten the novel published in the first place if she had not pretended to be a man.

Writing as George Eliot, Mary Ann went on to publish a number of other famous novels considered to be classics today. Those include *Mill on the Floss*, *Silas Marner*, *Daniel Deronda*, and her masterpiece, *Middlemarch*.

Mary Ann's novels provided an opportunity for her to talk about sexism in Victorian culture. In *Daniel Deronda*, one of her characters utters a line that must certainly have echoed Mary Ann's frustrations about being

FOUR FAMOUS WOMEN WRITERS (WHO WROTE UNDER MALE PEN NAMES)

1. Emily Brontë, author of *Wuthering Heights*, wrote under the name Ellis Bell.
2. Pearl S. Buck, author of *The Good Earth* and other works, sometimes wrote as John Sedges.
3. Amandine-Lucile-Aurore Dupin, a famous and prolific nineteenth-century French novelist, memoirist, and playwright, wrote as George Sand.
4. J.K. Rowling, author of the *Harry Potter* series, writes crime novels as Robert Galbraith.

SEVEN FUN FACTS ABOUT VICTORIANS

1. They were obsessed with death and mourning. They were very concerned about showing their mourning properly and even wrote books about how to do it right.
2. They liked tattoos.
3. They thought taxidermy was cool. They loved dead stuffed animals doing things like having tea parties or playing cricket.
4. They thought immersing people in hot or cold water could cure any disease. Hydrotherapy was a huge fad for a time.
5. They were fascinated by mummies.
6. They believed in hypnotism and would pay to see hypnotists perform in public.
7. They used arsenic in just about everything, from their makeup and shampoo to their dyes and wallpapers.

a woman: "You may try, but you cannot imagine what it is to have a man's force of genius in you, and to suffer the slavery of being a girl." Mary Ann wrote that line thirty years before the suffragette movement. She was clearly a woman ahead of her time.

As she got more and more famous, a curious thing happened: People stopped caring that she was living with George out of wedlock. Fame and money have a way of making people forget everything else.

Happy times couldn't last forever. George died in 1878, and Mary Ann was understandably devastated. He had been an important part of her literary career; he was her muse and her biggest champion. When Mary Ann was writing serialized novels, George often held back negative criticism because he knew Mary Ann might be deterred by negative letters. (Imagine if she had Twitter. Then she'd really know what it is like to be the victim of trolls.) George also made sure she had the time and space she needed to create brilliant work by taking care of day-to-day stuff. Without George, Mary Ann didn't know how to continue living and writing.

Her sadness over losing George was mitigated by a man named John Cross. He was an American banker who served as Mary Ann's business manager. Two years after George's death, Mary Ann married John. It was her first official marriage. Mary Ann was sixty-one then; John was just forty. Mary Ann was a cougar before it was fashionable!

Unfortunately, Mary Ann did not get to enjoy a long, happy marriage. Just months after marrying John, Mary Ann caught a cold. She died at the age of sixty-one. Her novels, though, would live on forever.

She is recognized as a major influence on nineteenth-century literature and is considered one of our greatest literary minds, all because she had the foresight to take a man's name in a world that believed women were inferior in every way. •

SECTION 3:
CHEATERS & THIEVES

History is full of cheats and thieves. Many made tons of money bilking innocent people out of their fortunes. Most ended up in jail. Some died penniless and alone in jail cells. Others managed to redeem themselves, but their names will always be associated with cheating.

Before you read about history's biggest cheaters and thieves, take this quiz to find out if you have ever pulled the kind of stunts these people have.

HOW BIG OF A CHEAT ARE YOU?

Answer the following questions by circling "yes" or "no."

1. Have you ever committed mail fraud, bilked people out of thousands of dollars, and then used the money to buy a mansion and gold-handled canes?
2. Have you ever sold a national landmark to a scrap metal dealer?
3. Have you ever convinced your friends to invest a whole lot of money in a scam?
4. Have you ever charged people to tell you their sins and promised God's forgiveness in return?
5. Have you ever convinced people you could talk to God for them?
6. Have you ever convinced people you could give supernatural powers to Japanese widows?
7. Have you ever cheated on a nationally televised quiz show?
8. Have you ever cheated in the Boston Marathon?
9. Have you ever cheated in the Tour de France?

If you answered **no** to all of these questions, good for you. You are not a cheater or a thief. You wouldn't dream of cheating your friends or strangers out of their hard-earned money. And you would never cheat at any game or contest. If you win, you'll do it fair and square.

If you answered **yes** to any of these questions, you are in trouble. In fact, how are you not in jail? You should probably re-think your life choices. Like the cheats in this chapter, you could end up alone and miserable. •

CHAPTER 9:
SLICK SALESMEN

THE LIAR:
CHARLES PONZI

DATE: 1920

THE LIE: That if people gave him money to invest, he could make them up to 400 percent more in interest

REASON: Because he could make millions running this scam

Imagine you go to school one day and ask your best friend Larry to give you ten dollars. In return, you promise to give Larry twenty dollars next week. Then Larry gets ten dollars from Curly and promises him fifteen dollars next week. Larry takes five dollars and gives you five. Then Curly asks Moe for ten dollars and promises him twelve dollars next week. Curly takes two dollars, Larry takes three dollars, and you take five dollars. If you keep the racket going, you will make a lot of money. Larry will make a little less. Curly, a little less than that. And so on. It's great for everyone until you get to the bottom of the chain. That person may very well end up with nothing.

The scam I just described is called a pyramid scheme. Pyramid schemes are illegal in the United States. That law is because of people like **Charles Ponzi**. Another name for a pyramid scheme is a Ponzi scheme. Charles ran a pyramid scheme that was so successful, he made more than $8,000,000 in eight months.

Charles was born Carlos Ponzi in Italy in 1882. Just five feet two inches tall, with cropped hair and a thick mustache, Carlos left his home when he was a young adult to study at the University of Rome. He dropped out because he was a bad student. He pre-ferred to make money.

Charles decided to leave Italy and go to Boston in 1903. He only had $2.50 in his pocket by the time he stepped off the ship. That's because he gambled away all his money

on the voyage to America. When he got off the ship, he dumped the name Carlos and became Charles.

Once in America, Charles knew he had to get a job. He ended up trying out lots of different gigs and different places to live. He was a busboy at a restaurant, a sign painter, a clerk to a broker, and a bank teller in Montreal, Canada. Unfortunately, the bank went broke, and Charles found himself, once again, with no money and prospects. To make ends meet, he wrote a bad check. He got caught and went to jail, but he was too ashamed to tell his mother back in Italy. He wrote her letters telling her he worked in a prison in Canada. Mrs. Ponzi bought it. She probably bragged to all her friends about her successful son.

After three years in Canadian jail, Charles moved back to the United States, where he started a business smuggling immigrants from Italy into the country. That landed him back in prison. Mrs. Ponzi again believed her boy was working in law enforcement. She was pretty gullible.

It took a woman to turn Charles around (although he didn't last long on the straight and narrow). He met Rose Gnecco, a stenographer, on a streetcar. They married in 1918. Rose's father owned a grocery store, so Mr. Gnecco hired Charles.

You probably won't be surprised when I tell you that Charles was not suited for the grocery business. (Charles wasn't really suited for anything that involved a lot of work.) While doing below-average work in the grocery story, Charles cooked up a plan to get rich. He decided to start an international trade journal and make money from advertising. The only problem was that he couldn't find anyone to give him a loan. (Mr. Gnecco undoubtedly decided his son-in-law was a bad financial risk.)

When a letter from Spain arrived, Charles knew he had his big idea. The letter included international reply coupons. These were coupons that could be exchanged for postage stamps in another country. Charles quickly figured out that he could buy international exchange coupons and then trade them for more expensive stamps in some other country. His new business was born. And, best of all, it didn't require a lot of work.

HUMBLE? NOT SO MUCH

Charles Ponzi might have been smart, but he wasn't exactly modest. He titled his 1936 autobiography *The Rise of Mr. Ponzi: The Long Suppressed Autobiography of a Financial Genius*.

FAMOUS PONZI SCHEMES

1. In 1880 Sarah Howe collected a "Ladies Deposit" and promised women an 8 percent return in their investment. She took the money and ran.
2. Michael Eugene Kelly bilked senior citizens out of more than $4,000,000 by promising them big payoffs for their investment in Cancun time-shares.
3. In the 1990s the Albanian government cheated citizens out of billions of dollars by running a number of Ponzi schemes. Not surprisingly, citizens overthrew the corrupt government, but most never received any money back.

Charles had people in other countries who would buy the coupons and send them to him. Then he would exchange them in the United States at a higher price. Then he could sell them. He knew if he could get some investors, he could make even more money. To entice investors, he offered 50 percent interest in just forty-five days. Investors were clamoring to give him money with return rates that high.

The stamp scheme was inspired by a man named William Miller. William was a Brooklyn bookkeeper who, in 1899, made more than $1,000,000 running a pyramid scheme. William's nickname was William "520 percent" Miller because he was known for increasing investments by 500 percent or more. Using the same pyramid structure, Charles made money just like William. He probably barely believed his good luck.

With all that cash rolling in, Charles bought a mansion with twelve rooms, a heated swimming pool, and air-conditioning. He paid for the house with $9,000 in cash and a Securities Exchange Company certificate that would be worth $30,000 in just a few months. He bought elegant and expensive jewels for Rose. He had his own limo. He even had a gold-handled walking stick. Charles was now the man he always wanted to be, not the grocery boy in Mr. Gnecco's rinky-dink shop.

You might think investors would be suspicious about handing over money to Charles. But they weren't because he was so smooth. His trick was to convince people he did *not* want their money. (That's some reverse psychology in action.) He would tell people that he wasn't accepting any additional investors, which made people want to invest even more. Charles would then reluctantly agree to take their money, but only, he would say, as a personal favor to them and because he didn't have time to mess around. He would claim to have important clients to meet, which made other people believe they were going to miss out on a deal that someone else would get. He refused to talk about business unless he was pressed, which made him look even more confident. Most of all, people believed in Charles because they wanted to. They desperately wanted to believe that they could get rich quick, just as Charles did.

Charles should have paid more attention to what happened to William, the pyramid schemer who inspired him. After making all that money, William ended up in Sing Sing where he became a new man and renounced his cheating ways. His new nickname was Honest Bill. Charles must have missed that part of the story. He was so high on his own success that he didn't believe he could ever be caught. He was wrong. A government auditor figured out what Charles was doing. A short investigation led to Charles's arrest.

In the summer of 1920, it seemed that everyone knew Charles's name. He was on the front page of all the Boston newspapers. And the fall of his Ponzi scheme was financially disastrous for everyone involved. Six banks failed. Many investors received only thirty cents on the dollar back on their investment. And those were the lucky ones. Some got nothing.

As for Charles, he went to jail for three and a half years. That's pretty generous considering he bilked people out of millions of dollars. While on parole, he went to Florida and was arrested for fraud, proving that he hadn't learned his lesson. He jumped bail, but he got caught in New Orleans. He went back to jail and wasn't released until 1934. At that point, he was deported back to Italy.

You might think he was sorry, but he wasn't. He believed he had given people something of value in spite of losing their money. He once said, "Even if they never got anything for it, it was cheap at that price... It was easily worth fifteen million bucks to watch me put the thing over."

Poor Rose's reputation was forever tarnished. She stood by Charles for a while, but she eventually grew tired of his antics. When he went back to Italy, she stayed in the United States She eventually divorced Charles and remarried. She probably hoped never to hear his name again.

Charles died in 1949 in Rio de Janeiro, Brazil. He was penniless. •

VICTOR LUSTIG

DATE: 1925

THE LIE: That he had been given permission by the French government to sell the Eiffel Tower for scrap metal

REASON: Because scrap metal is worth a lot of money

Born in what is now the Czech Republic in 1890, Robert V. Miller grew up to be a criminal mastermind who died penniless in a prison cell in Missouri. Most of his life he was known as **Victor Lustig**, and he ran such outrageous scams that you'll wonder how anyone ever fell for them.

Before he began his life of crime, Robert was just a normal kid from a middle-class family. His father was the mayor of the Czech town Hostinné. Robert graduated from high school and went on to the University of Paris. He was smart enough to do well, but he wasted his time (and money) gambling. He eventually left school and started committing a number of petty crimes. After hitting on another man's girlfriend, he walked away with a sizable scar on his cheek. That scar would become his trademark characteristic for the rest of his life.

After leaving the university in Paris, he dumped the name Robert and began going by the name Count Victor Lustig. Some say he was called "the Count" because he was so suave and sophisticated.

Victor was a decent gambler, so he spent significant time on cruise ships gambling and making money off rich people. He might have continued to make his living that way, but World War I happened, and the pleasure cruise industry came to a halt. Victor decided to come to the United States to try his luck at making money on land instead of on the sea.

Under the false name Robert Duval, Victor arrived in Missouri in 1922. He exchanged $22,000 in bonds to buy a ranch. Victor was so smooth that he convinced the bank teller to give him an additional $10,000 in cash to get the ranch up and running. He had his bonds in an envelope, and the bank teller put the cash in another envelope. By a clever sleight of hand, Victor managed to get both envelopes! He walked away with the bonds (which were probably not real in the first place) and thousands of dollars in cash. He didn't get far before he was arrested, but he managed to talk his way out of the charge. Somehow he convinced the cops that the situation was just a big mistake. The cops let him walk.

The bank incident taught Victor that he was going to have to get better at scamming people. In 1925, while in Paris, he had a bold idea: What if he could sell the Eiffel Tower? At the time, the tower was falling apart, and many Parisians thought it was an eyesore. The monument was left over from the 1889 Paris Exposition, and some citizens felt it was time to remove it since it had served its purpose. Others loved it and thought it should be kept and restored as the city's treasure. Victor decided to capitalize on this heated debate.

You might think that selling the Eiffel Tower would be a tough thing to do. Not for Victor. He pretended to be someone named Deputy Director General of the Ministère de Postes et Télégraphes. He then found his mark: André Poisson, a scrap metal dealer. Victor told André that he had been hired by the city to sell the tower for scrap metal. The only catch was that André couldn't tell a soul. Victor convinced him that Parisians who loved the tower would be livid if they knew what the French government was planning, so they had to keep the whole deal under wraps.

André was delighted to be offered a most excellent deal. All he had to do was pay $70,000 to Victor. Then, according to Victor, he would make sure the Parisian government chose André to haul away the tower. André could scrap all the metal and make back his $70,000 back plus a hefty profit. André thought this plan checked out, so he gave Victor the money and then quietly waited for the city of Paris to give him the signal. He probably stayed up late at night and counted all the money he would make.

With $70,000 in his pocket, Victor got out of Dodge and headed for Austria. (It was easy for Victor to travel extensively. He spoke fluent Czech, German, English, French, and Italian. Wherever he went, he could blend in.) He waited in Austria for the inevitable news that André had been fleeced. Victor assumed the French police would be after him, so he intended to stay far away from France. But a curious thing happened: No report came. That's because André never reported the crime! He was too embarrassed to tell anyone how easy it was for Victor to fleece him. André simply chalked up his loss as a very expensive lesson.

You might think that Victor would move on to a new scam, but he didn't. He had guts. He went back to Paris and pulled the trick again on another scrap dealer. This one seemed to fall for it, but Victor felt like something was a little bit off. He was right to be suspicious. This dealer called the police, but Victor was already one step ahead. He was long gone, on his way back to the United States.

The Eiffel Tower scam was clever, but Victor was full of clever ideas. In his cruise ships days, he used to sell little wooden boxes to unsuspecting passengers. He called his invention the Rumanian box, and he claimed it was a money duplication machine. All people had to do was put a crisp $100 bill into a small slot on one side. Then Victor would turn a crank. That would feed the bill into the box. Victor would then tell his skeptical audience that they needed to wait a few hours for "chemical processing." A few hours later, Victor would turn the crank and another $100 bill would pop out the other side. Rich cruise ship passengers were delighted by this oddity. They would even bid against each other to get their hands on this special wooden box. Victor would wisely wait until the end of the voyage, and then sell the box to the highest bidder. He could make anywhere from $10,000 to $30,000 for just one box.

You've probably figured out by now that Victor's wooden box was not a magic money-printing machine. It was another one of his scams. He would stuff the boxes with a few $100 bills before demonstrating its "magic" printing capabilities. By the time the rube who bought it figured out that it wasn't actually producing money, Victor would be long gone. And all it cost him was a few hundred dollars, money he made back in spades with the price of the box itself.

The famous mafia criminal, Al Capone, even had a run-in with Victor. Al lent Victor $50,000 for an unspecified business proposition. Victor promised to return the money plus $50,000 more. Curiously, Victor put the money away in a storage locker and came back two months later to say his scam fell through. He returned the original fifty grand to Al and apologized for his lack of profit. Al was so impressed with Victor's "honesty" that he gave him $5,000! Rumor has it that Victor simply wanted to earn Al's trust in case he ever needed a favor.

A criminal with many talents, Victor was an accomplished counterfeiter. When he was finally arrested, he had more than $50,000 in fake bills and printing plates stored in a locker in Times Square. Police took him

THIRTEEN COOL EIFFEL TOWER FACTS

1. The Eiffel Tower was originally constructed as an exhibition for the World's Fair in 1889. It was built to commemorate the centennial of the French Revolution and to celebrate modern science.
2. It was only supposed to stand for twenty years, but Paris decided to keep it.
3. There's an ice rink on the first level.
4. Maurice Koechlin and Émile Nouguier drew the original plans, but the credit went to Gustave Eiffel, the owner of the civil engineering firm for which Maurice and Emil worked.
5. The tower has more than 1,700 steps. (Don't worry: There's also an elevator.)
6. The tower required 18,000 individual parts to build it. Imagine getting done and finding one part leftover!
7. The tower cost 7,000,000 francs to build.
8. It took 300 workers to construct the tower.
9. The tower weighs 10,000 tons.
10. The tower expands in the sun. It can grow by up to 6.75 inches on a sunny day.
11. To keep the tower from rusting, workers apply sixty tons of paint every seven years.
12. Seven million people visit the tower every year.
13. It costs fifteen euros to go to the top of the tower. That's about $18.

to jail, but he escaped within hours. He used tied sheets to lower himself from his cell window and pretended to be a window washer. Passersby thought nothing of the man suspended outside the building.

You might wonder how he managed to get caught in the first place given that he was quite brilliant. His downfall was his girlfriend, Billy May. She found out he was cheating on her with another woman, so she called federal agents and turned him in.

He was eventually sentenced to fifteen years in prison, which wasn't such a bad sentence considering that he'd been arrested forty-five times in Europe alone and had escaped police more times than we can count in the United States.

In 1947 he died in a Missouri prison of either a brain tumor or pneumonia. His legacy lived on, though. For years after his death, his counterfeit money would occasionally turn up. Those bills were known as "Count Lustig money."

His death certificate listed his occupation as "salesman." That seems pretty accurate, but "crook" would have been more fitting. •

BERNIE MADOFF

DATE: Approximately 2000–2008
THE LIE: That he was investing friends' and strangers' money and bringing in high returns
REASON: To get even richer than he already was

You might remember when **Bernard "Bernie" Madoff** was arrested in December of 2008. After his arrest, he admitted that his asset management company was "just one big lie." He was running a scam that cost investors more than $65,000,000,000. That's sixty-five *billion*, mind you. To give you an idea how much money that is, think of it this way: Let's say that I have sixty-five billion to blow. And let's say you live to be 100 years old. If I give you $1,000,000 every day of your life until you die, I would still have $30,000,000,000 left for myself!

So how did Bernie manage to get his hands on more than $60,000,000,000 and lose it? He was running what's called a Ponzi scheme. (See the chapter on Charles Ponzi.) A Ponzi scheme is an illegal operation where one person takes money from "investors" and then uses other, later investors' money to pay the earlier investors. No money is really being made here. The person running the scam is just putting money in different hands, mainly his own.

A pyramid scheme, or a Ponzi scam, would be like if I asked you to invest a dollar with me. Let's say I can promise you a 12 percent return on your initial investment. So that's twelve cents. Then let's say I ask twenty other people to also give me a dollar, and I promise them the same return. When you decide to cash out your one dollar and take your profit, I give you one dollar and twelve cents from the later investors' money. It all works out great until everyone decides to cash out at the same time. And that's what happened to Bernie.

The stock market crashed in 2008, which frightened a lot of people. Suddenly, Bernie needed to pay out $7,000,000,000 really fast and he didn't have the money to do it. That's when the whole enterprise unraveled.

People were surprised to find out Bernie was a crook because he seemed like such an honest guy. He was an investment manager and ran a successful company called Madoff Investment Securities. He was wealthy in his later years, but he started out from a modest family in Queens, New York. It was hard to believe that someone who seemed so normal could be so vicious.

He was born in 1938 to Sylvia and Ralph Madoff. He went to the University of Alabama and later graduated from Hofstra University with a degree in political science. Though he was just an average student, he was an extremely hard worker. As a young man, he worked as a lifeguard and a sprinkler system salesman. He used the money he earned to trade penny

GET POOR QUICK!

MONEY DOWN THE TOILET

Bernie had a lot of victims. Some were ordinary people. Others were celebrities. But his biggest marks were huge corporations. Here are some of the organizations Bernie swindled along with the amount of money they lost.

- Fairfield Greenwich Advisers, $7 billion
- Royal Bank of Scotland, $492 million
- Fairfield, Connecticut (pension fund), $42 million
- New York University, $24 million
- The Elie Wiesel Foundation for Humanity, $15 million
- Korea Teachers Pension, $9 million
- Bard College, $3 million

stocks. In 1960, with $5,000 he'd managed to save, he started his company. He had an excellent financial mind, and he quickly became a Wall Street pioneer. He was one of the first and biggest proponents of electronic trading.

Bernie also had a successful personal life. He married Ruth Alpern, his high school sweetheart, and together they had three children. As Bernie's business grew more and more successful, the couple bought houses all over the world, including one on Long Island, one in Palm Springs, and one in the south of France. Ruth spent her time volunteering for charities and decorating their homes while Bernie filled the bank accounts.

In spite of their incredible wealth, the Madoffs were pretty down-to-earth. When the Madoffs were in New York, they loved to dine at a small Italian restaurant called Primola. Bernie always ordered a salad, chicken scarpiello, and a Diet Coke. That's hardly the dinner of someone who literally had billions of dollars to spend.

Friends of Bernie described as him quiet, polite, and dependable, but they did admit he was sometimes a bit of a strange ranger. He wouldn't let anyone in his company use blue pens. All pens had to be black. He once ripped out carpet in his offices because of a small pear juice stain in a one area. While both of those things might suggest he was a little weird, they don't suggest that he was a dirty thief, which he also was.

While running his legitimate company, Bernie was running his Ponzi scheme on the side. He operated the illegal company on a separate floor of his office building. He traveled often and met wealthy people all over the world. He seemed so smart and sincere that he could convince people to invest millions of dollars with him. Every month, he sent statements to his clients telling them they were making 10 or 12 percent returns. Those aren't super-high numbers, so they didn't raise any red flags. What eventually did cause suspicion was that Bernie's returns were so consistent. That level of consistency was unheard of.

Though Bernie's consistent rates were dubious, people kept "investing" with him. They trusted him because he seemed to know what he was doing and was always kind. He would frequently tell little old ladies that their money was safe with him because he wouldn't dream of scamming them. He was so honest seeming that he earned the trust of multiple charities, celebrities, and banks.

Part of the reason he seemed so trustworthy was that he had his legitimate business in place, so he could come up with cash when his "investors" wanted out. As long as the majority of them kept their money with him, he could keep the scam going, building more and more of a fortune for himself.

The Securities and Exchange Commission (SEC) investigated Bernie before he was eventually arrested in 2008. What he gave them was a set of "cooked books." That means he kept false records that made it look like he was really investing money, not just shifting money from one person to another. The SEC basically took one look at the cooked books and said, "Okay, looks good." Bernie himself was surprised that they didn't investigate further or ask for hard proof.

CELEBRITY VICTIMS

Bernie knew a lot of celebrities, and he wasn't afraid to take their money. Zsa Zsa Gabor, a famous actress, lost $10,000,000. Other celebrity victims include the following people:

- Stephen Spielberg, film director
- Larry King, talk show host
- Kevin Bacon, actor
- Uma Thurman, actress
- Eliot Spitzer, former New York state attorney general
- Sandy Koufax, retired baseball player

The scam might have gone on a lot longer, but Bernie knew he was stuck when he had just $300,000,000 left and he needed to pay out billions of dollars. He confessed to his two sons, who called the FBI. Bernie then confessed to an FBI agent named Theodore Cacioppi. Theodore wondered if maybe there was an "innocent explanation," but Bernie was forced to admit his lie. He told Theodore he was running "a giant Ponzi scheme."

Many of Bernie's victims lost all their money. Sondra Weiner, for example, and her son had to sell all their assets, including their homes. They had no idea that Bernie had basically stolen their fortune until they were presented with a zero balance. Think that's cold? Well, Sondra is Bernie's sister and her son is Bernie's nephew. Even Bernie's family wasn't safe from his lies! It was hard for many people to believe that someone who seemed like such a nice guy could be so cold and ruthless. This man whom everyone thought was so kind and polite was stealing from anyone who trusted him.

At seventy years old, he was sentenced to 150 years in prison. His brother, Peter, was sentenced to ten years. His sons, who claimed they didn't know Bernie was running a scam, didn't fare well even though they were never arrested. Mark killed himself two years after Bernie's arrest. Andrew died of blood cancer recently. Ruth, Bernie's wife, divorced him and is still alive, but she doesn't have anything to do with Bernie. She was forced to give up more than $100,000,000,000 in property and assets. That's a lot of zeroes. No wonder she's teed off with Bernie.

Not surprisingly, a lot of people hate Bernie. There's even a hot sauce called "Bernie in Hell" in honor of him. Mention Bernie Madoff to just about anybody, and you might hear that he's a dirty, no-good crook who deserves to rot in a fiery place.

He's currently in a medium-security prison, but he isn't well. He recently had a heart attack, and he suffers from advanced stages of kidney disease.

Bernie said it best himself: "I have left a legacy of shame." •

CHAPTER 10:
RELIGIOUS SCAMMERS

LEO X

DATE: 1513–1521
THE LIE: That he could forgive sins if you paid him the right price
REASON: To finish building a cathedral (among other things)

Giovanni de' Medici was born in 1475 in Florence, Italy. His father was an important political leader named Lorenzo the Magnificent. (What an awesome name, right?) Giovanni was the second son, which meant he was turned over to the Catholic Church to be a priest. He became a monk at the age of seven and a deacon at the age of thirteen. At just thirty-seven years old, he became the pope. His new name was **Pope Leo X**.

Leo replaced Pope Julius II, who loved war; in fact, war was basically Julius II's favorite thing in life. Leo, on the other hand, had less deadly interests. His favorite hobby was spending money. He had a top-notch education and he loved books, so he spent tons of money buying books for the Vatican Library. He also liked culture, so he spent a lot of money on bringing plays, ballets, music, and games to the Vatican. He enjoyed serving his guests expensive dishes, like peacock tongue. (That's a real thing, by the way. It supposedly tastes like pheasant.)

You don't always think about popes being funny, but Leo was a fan of comedy. He liked having clowns around all the time (which seems more terrifying than funny). He was particularly amused by comedy that involved food. For instance, he liked to serve surprise desserts. Servants would cut a pie and birds would fly out of it. Sometimes the cooks would make a giant pastry and children would jump out of it. (Keep in mind I said he liked comedy, but I never said he liked sophisticated comedy. If Leo were alive now, he might be a fan of *Jackass* movies.)

When he wasn't at the Vatican with his clowns, Leo was out hunting at his country estate. He was gone for six weeks a year trudging through his hunting lands. One wonders who did all the pope work then.

An art lover, Leo financed the artist Raphael. Supporting an artist as a patron was a common practice at the time. The artist would make art in exchange for living expenses. Leo loved Raphael's artistic mind, and he wanted him to paint St. Peter's Basilica, a very expensive church that was being built. Raphael knew which side his bread was buttered on: He frequently painted Leo's face in his depictions of heroes and saints. Leo kept paying him.

As you can see, living like Leo took a lot of funds. It's no surprise then that he bankrupted the Church's treasury in just eight years. And St. Peter's, the cathedral, wasn't even close to finished. Leo couldn't bear to see the church unfinished, and he certainly didn't want to change his lifestyle. He liked having tons of money. Who wouldn't? Leo came from a sophisticated and wealthy family, and he wasn't about to start living in poverty now that he was head of the most powerful church in the world. On top of that, he was also the ruler of the Papal States and the Florentine Republic as head of the Medici family. (His father and older brother were dead by now.)

What do you do when you need a lot of cash fast? If you are Pope Leo X, you bring back something called an indulgence. An indulgence was something a Catholic could buy in exchange for forgiveness. Going to confession (or penance) required people to admit their sins, but they were still subject to a punishment. An indulgence took the place of a punishment. Instead of fasting or saying a million prayers, you could just buy your way out of your sin. In addition, an indulgence could cover a sin that you were just *thinking* about. So if you spent all of fifth-period Latin thinking about

stealing Nero's toga, an indulgence would take care of any punishment. It was brilliant, frankly.

Leo profited from indulgences, but he didn't invent them. Julius II handed them out too. In fact, they had been popular since the eleventh century. What Leo did do was make indulgences even more sought after. He told his flock of believers that indulgences could decrease the amount of time you spent in purgatory. Purgatory was a place somewhere between heaven and hell. You had to earn a certain number of prayers to get out of purgatory and move on to heaven. Indulgences could decrease your purgatory time. Even better, you could buy indulgences for dead relatives and move them out faster too.

Bringing indulgences back to the Church was a smart move for Leo. All he had to do was provide a signed document in exchange for the money he needed to maintain his lavish lifestyle. Beginning in 1517 he offered indulgences for anyone who "donated" money to St. Peter's. In that way, he kept the building schedule moving right along *and* continued to live the life of the super-rich.

CRAZIEST POPES

Leo X might have been a bad pope, but he wasn't the worst pope ever. And he certainly wasn't the craziest. Check out the truly bonkers things these popes did.

1. Pope Stephen VI dug up the corpse of the previous pope, Pope Formosus, and put him on trial. Formosus was found guilty, so Stephen ordered his fingers cut off. You should know that Formosus had been dead for nine months already when his trial began.
2. Pope Sergius III didn't like Formosus either. He got hold of his body and cut off his head. Sergius did this in addition to fathering a child from a teenage girl. That child grew up to be a pope himself!
3. Alexander VI married his own daughter off three times in order to get money and power.
4. Pope John XII had a fair number of mistresses, but that's not the worst thing he did. He also ran a house of prostitution from one of his palaces. (He was beaten to death by an angry husband.)
5. Pope Benedict IX sold the pope position twice in order to make some extra cash. He also married his cousin.

Soon Leo figured out that he could make more money if he sold indulgences beyond the Papal States (Italy). So he got priests all over Europe to preach about indulgences. Johann Tetzel, a German, was an enthusiastic priest who was very good at selling indulgences. People all over Germany were excited to send money off to Rome for Leo to spend. The practice caught the attention of someone who would go on to become very famous, someone who would change the fate of the Catholic Church forever. That person was Martin Luther, the founder of the Reformation and the namesake of the Lutheran Church.

Martin thought indulgences were a gross misuse of the Church's power. He started questioning Leo's finances and his theology. Roman officials worried about Martin's influence, but Leo brushed him off. He was more interested in his new hobby: planning a crusade. Leo wanted to send Catholics to Turkey to fight (and convert) Muslims. Someone who signed up for a crusade would be given a cross from Leo, and then he would be considered a soldier. Crusading had the added benefit of earning indulgences. How much of an indulgence one received was based on how much money one had. Of course.

Money from all over Europe was going directly to Rome, and that irritated Martin. He pointed out that Germany would be better off if people spent their money in their own country rather than sending it to Rome to be given to Leo. Germans decided Martin was right. Leo's popularity in Germany plummeted.

Martin and others also raised valid questions about where all the money being sent to Leo was going. Leo never launched a crusade, even though he was always planning one. St. Peter's remained unfinished, even though building continued. Poor people remained poor. The only person who had money, seemingly, was Leo himself!

Leo scoffed at Martin's concerns. Leo said there was absolutely nothing wrong with indulgences. "There are many," he declaimed, "and there will be many, who will gladly purchase eternal life for a small price, if they see that others are fighting for God in earnest, rather than pretending to do so." Oh, sick burn, Leo.

Eventually, Martin issued his ninety-five theses (or statements) on indulgences. These statements led to the Protestant Reformation, the greatest split in the Catholic Church in its history. Some historians think that if Leo had taken Martin more seriously, the Reformation may never have happened. When Leo died in 1521, he left the Church and the city in turmoil.

Some might argue that Leo didn't so much as lie as mislead people. We can't definitively prove that purgatory does or doesn't exist, nor can we prove that indulgences work or not. But Leo specifically increased the sale of indulgences in order to continue to buy giant pies with live children in them. That alone suggests that he wasn't selling God's forgiveness for the good of humankind so much that he really, really wanted more peacock tongue for dinner. •

SUN MYUNG MOON

DATE: 1980s

THE LIE: That he reported all of his income to the federal government.

REASON: To fund his empire

The 1960s and '70s ushered into the United States a number of worldwide religious movements. One of this movements was the Unification Church, started by **Sun Myung Moon**, a Korean man who believed Jesus had appointed him savior of humanity. In 1992 he officially declared himself the messiah. That's right. *The* messiah. Sun had some seriously high self-esteem.

Sun Myung was born in 1920 in what is now North Korea. At the age of ten, his family converted to Presbyterianism. As a young adult, he moved to Japan to attend college, where he majored in electrical engineering. After graduation he moved to Pyongyang (now the capital of North Korea) and started the Kwang-ya Church. The government didn't like that at all, so it threw him in prison and charged him with polygamy. Sun Myung claimed he was beaten and tortured in prison.

Eventually, Sun Myung was released and went to South Korea, and it was there that he started the Unification Church. The church still exists today, and members are known as Moonies. (The name was originally meant to be derisive, but it caught on and now that's how the church is known by most people.)

The Unification Church is based on a number of existing philosophies, including Christianity, Confucianism (an Eastern religion), anti-communist ideology, and a little bit of shamanism (an Eastern spiritual practice designed to contact the spirit world).

Although the church has strong roots in other religious philosophies, Sun Myung's reason for starting the church might seem a little bit wacko. He believed that Eve had an affair with Satan before she married Adam.

Eve's indiscretion, according to Sun Myung, was the reason the world was in such a sorry state. He believed that he was the perfect Adam and therefore the only person who could reform society. After the reformation happened, South Korea would then lead the world to a state of perfect grace. Easy peasy.

Marriage was a central component of Sun Myung's philosophy because he believed that marriage was necessary for our salvation. To this day, his church still arranges unions between young people. Think Match.com but done by Sun Myung (or some other church official) and some brief questionnaires administered to young singles.

Once matches are made, a church official marries these people in mass wedding ceremonies. In fact, those wedding ceremonies are what Sun Myung first became famous for. In 1982 he married 2,000 couples in Madison Square Garden in New York. In 2009 he married 5,000 couples in Seoul, South Korea.

After the marriage ceremonies, Sun Myung required each individual couple to spend three days engaged in — well, how do I put this — *intimate* acts. Even stranger, he required those acts to happen in front of a giant portrait of him! He wanted his followers to be thinking of him even when they were doing it. Weird, right?

Sun Myung's obsession with marriage came from his theology. Because Jesus died before marrying and having kids, Sun Myung believed it was his duty to ensure that he helped humanity complete that procreative mission; indeed, he believed that marriage was the *only* important mission in life. Everything else was inconsequential.

Sun Myung's ideas about eternal marriage, however, provided some rather large loopholes for himself. He divorced his first wife and married his second wife when he was forty years old and she was seventeen. Her name was Hak Ja Han, and she was the daughter of his cook. Sun Myung kept Hak Ja in a room for the first three years of marriage to purify her. They went on to have fourteen children.

In its early days, the Unification Church required a lot of money to operate. The Moon family also required a lot of money to live in the lap of luxury. That's because Sun Myung was said to treat his children like little gods, often requiring his followers to care for them so that he and his wife could enjoy their fabulous wealth. The Moon family lived in a mansion in New York situated on eighteen acres. The house had a ballroom, a bowling alley, and a dining room outfitted with a pond and waterfall. The kitchen had six pizza ovens. (The Moons obviously really liked pizza.)

Where did all this money come from? Well, it came from the church's followers, who were encouraged to donate their money to support the church. In addition, Sun Myung's followers would stand on street corners and in airports selling flowers. Reportedly, some went to Japan to sell small trinkets to Japanese widows for huge sums of money. Here's how it worked: Church members would tell widows that if they bought a small statue of a pagoda (a temple), then their dead husbands would be released from eternal punishment. By some estimates, Sun Myung made millions of dollars from these poor Japanese widows alone! (Moon denies such a thing.)

To truly grow an empire though, Sun Myung needed billions of dollars. To do that, he invested in just about every industry you can imagine: newspapers, hotels, sports teams, schools, hospitals, recording studios, and

[WARNING! MANDATORY FART JOKE BELOW]

POOT!

even jewelry markets. Some of the money went to running the church, but much of it went to Sun Myung's lavish lifestyle. One report suggests that Sun Myung's children could buy whatever they wanted whenever they wanted. Sun Myung himself was very active in conservative politics and frequently used money from his businesses to push his political agenda.

One of Sun Myung's largest sources of income was his seafood distribution company. It still exists today and supplies almost every sushi restaurant in the United States. Sun Myung correctly believed that seafood would be the ticket to unimaginable wealth. In 1980 he delivered a sermon outlining his plan. That sermon was called "The Way of Tuna." His company was so successful that he named himself the "King of the Ocean."

Interestingly, Sun Myung's fish empire benefited from his church's mass marriages. You see, the United States government forbade open-sea fishing beyond 200 miles from shore unless you were an American citizen. Sun Myung easily overcame that obstacle by marrying Americans to Japanese. Then they could fish just about anywhere.

The self-proclaimed King of the Ocean claimed that his operation would end world hunger. More than thirty years later, Sun Myung's company continues to provide fish to sushi restaurants in all fifty states, but world hunger still exists. In reality, his enormous wealth benefited him and his family. Eradicating world hunger was a just a clever lie to make him look noble.

The Unification Church has faced its fair share of public relations problems. In 1981 Sun Myung was indicted on twelve counts of tax fraud. He was convicted and sentenced to eighteen months in prison. The Japanese

CHILDREN OF THE MOON

Sun Myung and his wife gave most of their children Korean and American names. Here's a list of their fourteen kids.

- Ye Jin
- Hyo Jin (Stephen)
- Hye Jin
- In Jin (Tatiana)
- Heung Jin (Richard)
- Un Jin (Christina)
- Hyun Jin (Preston)
- Kook Jin (Justin)
- Kwon Jin (Nathaniel)
- Sun Jin (Tiffany, Salina)
- Young Jin (Phillip)
- Hyung Jin (Sean)
- Yeon Jin (Kat)
- Jeung Jin (Victoria)

widow scam didn't help to change the public perception of the church as a giant cult. In the 1980s many families of church members would have their loved one "kidnapped" and sent to deprogramming facilities.

One of the biggest Unification Church scandals happened more recently when Sun Myung's daughter took over for her ailing father. In Jin — whose American name is Tatiana — believed that the church was too old-fashioned. In 2010 she took over the services and used the time to talk about her passions, one of whom is Liberace (a famous performer and pianist). In Jin wanted to attract more young people to the church, so she changed the name to Lovin' Life Ministries. She encouraged young adults to join in Ping-Pong games and *Guitar Hero* tournaments. She even created a band called Sonic Cult to play at church services.

In Jin's plan to attract more people didn't work. Service attendance fell from more than 25,000 people to under 10,000. Old people were particularly ticked off. They referred to In Jin's changes as evidence of her "bling-bling style." And that wasn't a compliment.

In 2012 In Jin simply disappeared. She didn't even show up for her father's funeral. The reason for her disappearance came to light later: She was pregnant with her boyfriend's child. Like most of the Moon children, In Jin was forced into an arranged marriage. She left her husband and moved in with her boyfriend, the lead singer of Sonic Cult.

Sun Myung Moon died at the age of ninety-two. He had pneumonia and severe kidney problems. The man who named himself "True Father" lives on through the Unification Church. Membership numbers are low today, but church members exist across the entire world.

And just think: Every time you eat sushi, you are indirectly supporting the King of the Ocean. •

PETER POPOFF

DATE: 1980s
THE LIE: That he was a psychic
REASON: To collect money from his parishioners

The 1980s was a strange decade. Not only was it a time of big hair, shoulder pads, and neon colors, but it was also the decade of televangelists and faith healers. The airwaves were full of preachers who claimed they could cure any illness, often by just touching the afflicted.

Peter Popoff was one of those preachers. As well as claiming he had healing powers, he told his flock he was psychic. People would come to his services hoping to be pulled from the audience. If they were, Peter would tell them all sorts of private information about their lives and their illnesses. He claimed God was giving him this blessed power of "prophetic anointing." Pretty cool.

Peter was born in 1946 in Germany. When he was young, his family moved to California. In 1970 he married a woman named Elizabeth and they started a church in California. That church grew until Peter and Elizabeth were making thousands of dollars a month. At the height of Peter's popularity, in the '80s, his monthly church budget was more than $500,000 (that was a lot in 1980s dollars). He was broadcast on fifty-one television outlets and more than forty radio stations.

People from all over the country came to see Peter live at one of his services in the hopes of being healed. During the service, Peter would call out personal details that matched someone in the congregation. That person would stand up and come to the stage. Then Peter would "heal" them. Sounds nifty, right?

It sounded fishy to James Randi. James is a famous skeptic and magician who made it his mission to figure out how Peter was pulling off this stunt. James and his team of researchers went to one of Peter's services at the San Francisco Civic Center. They brought with them a very expensive piece of equipment that could detect frequencies. It didn't take long for their machine to stop at 39.17 megahertz. That's where they heard his wife, Elizabeth, feeding lines directly into Peter's ear through an earpiece. (Peter claimed to wear a hearing aid, but that raises another question: Why didn't he heal himself?) Peter wasn't hearing the voice of God. He was hearing his wife telling him details that their staff had collected from the audience prior to the service.

James and his team heard Elizabeth telling Peter (whom Elizabeth calls "Petey") when she had a "hot one" for him. A hot one would be someone in desperate need of a medical miracle. With Elizabeth's information, Peter could pretend that God was telling him that he had the power to heal. It didn't matter that Peter didn't heal these people. What mattered is people believed he had a direct line to God.

Peter was clearly a fraud, but James and his team decided to gather more information to really stick it to the guy. They went to other services and planted fake "hot ones" in the audience. As the skeptics predicted, Elizabeth fed Peter names of these planted parishioners with made-up ailments. At one service, Elizabeth recognized a man who had come to a previous show. This time he was dressed as a woman with an entirely new identity. Elizabeth practically blew out Peter's eardrum as she warned him to abort immediately.

After gathering enough information to prove beyond a shadow of a doubt that Peter was a big fat liar, James decided to break the news in a strange way: He went on *The Tonight Show* with Johnny Carson. (This was long before Jimmy Fallon hosted the show.) James played the tapes and told everyone exactly how Peter was fooling his blindly trusting followers. He explained to Johnny and all the at-home viewers that Peter and Elizabeth collected this information by asking people to fill out prayer cards on their way into a service. People would spill their guts right there on paper. All Elizabeth had to do was read the cards to Peter. And all Peter had to do was pretend he was concentrating really hard to get transmissions from heaven.

The big reveal on a national television show should have been the last anybody ever saw of Peter. But that's not what happened. He denied lying at first. Then, when he realized there was too much evidence against him, he claimed that his broadcasts were like a game show. I'm not sure how that makes what he did better, but that's what he said. And a lot of people were okay with that excuse.

LIFESTYLES OF THE RICH AND RELIGIOUS

Peter Popoff was certainly not the first (nor the last) televangelist to steal believers' money. Check out these televangelists who have allegedly taken millions of dollars from faithful supporters and lived like kings. Since their ministries have nonprofit status, they are not required to pay taxes on their earnings.

1. Oral Roberts once asked for millions of dollars in donations to keep God from taking him from this earth. In his later years he owned multiple houses, a jet, and a lot of fancy jewelry. (But he made sure to have his diamond rings airbrushed out of publicity photos.)
2. Pat Robertson sold an energy drink that he claimed was so effective that it helped him leg-press an incredible 2,000 pounds. He allegedly owns a diamond mine in Africa.
3. Paul and Janice Crouch received a memo of concern from their granddaughter, who claims her grandparents' Trinity Broadcasting Network violated IRS tax codes. (Paul and Janice deny the charges.) The Crouches have a private jet and thirteen mansions. They reportedly have a $100,000 RV just for their dogs. Some sources say they spend more than $300,000 a year just for dinners.
4. Benny Hinn, a self-proclaimed faith healer who claims to have seen a dead man resurrected, once sent a letter to his followers asking them to donate money to to help him get out of debt. They did it. He allegedly lives in a $10,000,000 home near the Pacific Ocean and owns multiple cars.
5. Joyce Meyer takes in millions of dollars in donations from her followers. Sources say she has a private jet, multiple vehicles, and five homes for herself and her children. Joyce says God made her rich.

The psychic bit wasn't the only project Peter started in the '80s that didn't quite turn out the way he hoped it would. In 1985 he decided to buy a bunch of Bibles, tie tiny helium balloons to them, and dump them out of a rented 747 jet over the Soviet Union. You can probably find at last two problems with this plan. Not only would Bibles need a whole lot of little parachutes to allow them to gently float into the hands of some deserving person, but the Soviet Union probably wouldn't have looked kindly on an unauthorized jet doing flyovers. Nevertheless, Peter asked people to donate money. And they did! One old woman gave away her entire life savings of $21,000.

Peter had no trouble finding followers. His church assistants would send thousands of "letters" to real people. Those letters appeared to be personally typed or handwritten. (Sometimes the letters included both typed and cursive messages.) Peter was actually using a computer to print these letters, but it was the '80s, and many people didn't know a computer could do such things. The perceived personal touch made it easier for Peter to recruit members.

Things did get rough for Peter, at least for a little while. In 1986, shortly after the Johnny Carson episode aired, Peter had to declare bankruptcy. But you know what? That didn't stop Peter. Your jaw is going to drop when I tell you that he kept preaching and went on to raise millions of dollars. His church is making millions today, in fact. Even after being revealed as a fraud, he's still collecting money from innocent believers.

How did Peter survive a very public unveiling of his lies? He did what any good liar does: He came up with a new scam. Today you might see Peter on the BET network, where he sells sacred water that will eliminate all your financial debt. You read that right. For just a few dollars, you can send away for Peter's magic water. It comes in a little vial, and all you have to do is drink and wait for your bank account to grow. Peter sends the

EMBARRASSING SCANDALS

Televangelists are no strangers to scandals. Here are some of the biggest ones that have happened in the last thirty years. Most involve money or sex.

1. Jimmy Swaggert was caught with a prostitute.
2. Bob Moorehead was arrested for indecent exposure in a public bathroom in Florida. Though charges were eventually dropped, Bob has admitted to other improprieties.
3. Kent Hovind was convicted of more than fifty federal tax offenses.
4. Ted Haggard visited prostitutes and took meth.
5. Gilbert Deya has been accused of selling Kenyan babies to infertile couples.
6. W.V. Grant went to jail for tax fraud.

water for free, but he strongly encourages you to send a donation in return. Somebody out there must be sending him money because his income is more than what most people will make in twenty years, let alone one.

Since the Johnny Carson debacle, other national reporters and major television shows (like *Inside Edition*) have done stories on him. It doesn't seem to matter. People love Peter and continue to give him money. He's like a rubber ball: He always bounces back.

Peter preaches that God wants people to be debt-free. If that's true, it seems that God wants Peter to be the most debt-free of us all. •

CHAPTER 11:
CHEATERS NEVER WIN (EXCEPT WHEN THEY DO)

CHARLES VAN DOREN

DATE: 1956–1957
THE LIE: That he knew answers to questions on a popular television quiz show
REASON: Because the producers wanted him to win

In the 1950s television producers were looking for ways to provide entertaining programming without spending a lot of money. Inspired by a trivia game called *The $64 Question* on the popular 1940s radio program *Take It or Leave It*, producers came up with an idea for a TV game show. In June 1955 that game show debuted in homes across America. It was called *The $64,000 Question*. The premise was simple: Players started at just one dollar and doubled their winnings every time they answered a question correctly. The show was so popular that scores of similar programs emerged. In the 1957–1958 television season alone, twenty-two quiz shows were airing during the day or in primetime.

It's pretty safe to say that American TV viewers in the '50s loved their game shows. Part of what viewers loved was the drama of returning contestants. They tuned in day after day to see if their favorite contestant could keep his or her winning streak going. Audiences thrilled at hearing questions that required obscure knowledge and discovering that beloved contestants knew the answers.

So imagine how upset viewers were when they learned that quiz shows — not just one of them, but almost all of them — were rigging the games. One contestant would go down in history as the most famous quiz show cheater, a reputation that would follow him his entire life.

Charles Van Doren was thirty years old when a friend of his mentioned that he had been on a popular game show called *Tic-Tac-Dough*. Charles thought that going on a game show sounded like an easy way to make some money. He was an English instructor at Columbia University in New York at the time and was making just a little over $4,000 a year. He didn't even own a TV. Nevertheless, Charles found his way onto a popular quiz show called *Twenty One*.

The producers at *Twenty One* were excited to find Charles. He was young and reasonably attractive. He was likable, and he was the sort of guy people could root for. On top of that, he had an interesting family. His father, Mark Van Doren, was a poet. His mother, Dorothy Van Doren, was a novelist. And his uncle, Carl Van Doren, was a famous Pulitzer Prize–winning historian. The producers knew that they'd found a person who would inspire audiences to tune in week after week.

On December 5, 1956, Charles made his small-screen debut. He was put up against a man named Herb Stempel. Herb had won $70,000 over the course of six weeks, but his popularity was waning with audiences. Charles was the perfect contestant to get rid of Herb.

Now before you feel too sorry for Herb, you should know that he'd been fed answers by producers for weeks. Even his appearance had been altered to appeal to the audience. Producers had asked him to wear an ill-fitting suit and appear nervous. They wanted him to seem like a poor student. In reality, he was married to a wealthy woman who once had to be kicked off the set when she showed up wearing a fur stole! On air, Herb would stand in the isolation booth and pretend to be thinking hard to come up with answers. Sometimes the booth was made hotter just to get a couple of extra beads of sweat on his brow.

But producers (and audience) grew tired of sweaty Herb. It was time for his winning streak to end. Producers gave Charles the answers and told him he was the next star. Herb wasn't happy about that, but producers told him he wouldn't get any money if he didn't comply. Audiences were thrilled when, after a tie, Charles finally won. The tie, of course, was scripted. Producers wanted audiences to keep tuning in for the nail-biting drama.

As the network hoped, the ratings for *Twenty One* increased, so they let Charles keep winning. Keep in mind that they were still giving him the

THE QUIZ SHOW MOVIE

In 1994 Robert Redford directed a movie about the 1950s quiz show scandals. The movie was called *Quiz Show*. Actor Ralph Fiennes played Charles Van Doren. Herb Stempel was played by John Turturro, who later went on to be in the *Transformers* movies.

answers beforehand. In fact, the show was scripting just about everything, including *how* Charles answered questions. He even rehearsed his answers before the show to ensure that audiences would find him believable. His work paid off: Viewers absolutely loved him. He received around 500 fan letters a week. (Think about that for a second: About 500 people a week were writing letters on paper with pens and pencils and mailing them off. To a game show contestant. Can you imagine people taking the time to do that now?)

By January of 1957, Charles was up to $100,000 in winnings. He was so charming that viewers weren't tired of him yet. They were particularly delighted when he beat Edgar Cummings, a former college president. Charles beat Edgar by answering some super-obscure questions. Instead of being suspicious, audiences assumed he was brilliant. It seemed like Charles was going to win the game forever.

Not surprisingly, Charles didn't win forever. The network and the producers understood that watching Charles win would get boring eventually. To keep the audiences excited, they had to throw in some unexpected moves. So on February 11, 1958, with $138,000 in his bank account, Charles tied a lawyer named Vivienne Nearing. She went on to beat him in subsequent rounds. And when I say she beat him, I mean that the producers instructed him to give the wrong answers. So many viewers tuned in for the big showdown that the game show beat *I Love Lucy* in the ratings. That was a very big deal. *Lucy* was the most popular show on TV, and viewers were very loyal to it.

In spite of his loss, TV viewers still wanted more Charles. He signed a contract with NBC for $150,000 to appear on multiple talk shows. He was even given a correspondent position on *The Today Show*. He appeared on the cover of *Time*. Charles was everywhere, and he was a bona fide Hollywood personality.

Cheating was so rampant on quiz shows that audiences eventually started to suspect what was happening. And they didn't like feeling like dupes.

YOU CAN'T FOOL BOB REDFORD

Robert Redford claims that he knew Charles Van Doren was just pretending to know the answers to the questions when he saw the actual game show. Robert was in film school at the time.

ANOTHER FAMOUS GAME SHOW CONTESTANT

Charles Van Doren was certainly famous as a game show contestant, but years later another quiz show contestant went on to be even more famous. And this contestant wasn't cheating. Ken Jennings — using nothing but his smarts — won $2,500,000 in a seventy-two-game winning streak on *Jeopardy!* He lost on a question about H&R Block, a tax preparation company.

The legal system had to get involved. Charles was questioned by a district attorney and a grand jury, but he denied that the show rigged anything. He even said this: "It's silly and distressing to think that people don't have more faith in quiz shows." Charles was lying through his teeth! And for good reason, I suppose. He knew if he admitted what was happening on these quiz shows, he'd lose his fancy new jobs and be forever known as a liar and a cheat.

In 1959 he realized he couldn't keep lying. There were too many people coming forward about the ubiquitous quiz show scandals. NBC fired him immediately, of course. He also had to resign from Columbia. His name was so well known that he couldn't go anywhere without people know he was *the* Charles Van Doren, the man who cheated on a game show and knowingly fooled millions of viewers.

On top of that, Charles was in some pretty serious legal trouble for lying to a grand jury. He pled guilty to second-degree perjury (which is lying). That's a misdemeanor crime, so he didn't go to jail. Nobody went to jail for the quiz scandals. At least a hundred contestants lied to the grand jury, but only seventeen were indicted and arrested. (Interestingly, Herb, the guy in the bad suit whom Charles first beat, was the first person on *Twenty One* to admit to cheating. The show claimed he was the first person they'd asked to cheat.)

The quiz show scandals rocked the TV world for years afterward. Viewers wanted assurance that what they were seeing was real and not dramatized for the screen. Can you imagine what viewers of the 1950s would think about reality TV now? Almost everything we see on TV is scripted, yet we're told over and over again that what we see is "reality." In the '50s, that wouldn't fly. People wanted the real deal.

As for Charles, he's doing okay. He's still alive. He and his wife, Gerry, are both college professors. He also worked for years as an editor for *Encyclopedia Britannica*. Charles has enjoyed a long and successful writing career, though he wrote under a pseudonym to avoid readers associating his writing with his quiz show scandal. That is perhaps a different sort of lie.

Still, Charles Van Doren will go down in history, not as a smart and hardworking man with many talents, but as a quiz show cheater. It's true that Charles did lie, but remember that he was young and dumb. He was offered a whole lot of money to answer questions on TV, and it probably seemed like no big deal at the time.

Maybe we can muster a little sympathy for Charles. We might have done the same thing. •

ROSIE RUIZ

DATE: April 21, 1980
THE LIE: That she ran the Boston Marathon in a record-setting time
REASON: She wanted to win the race without running

Let's start with a little math. Stick with me here for a second. A marathon is 26.2 miles. In 1980 **Rosie Ruiz** seemed to have finished the Boston Marathon in two hours, thirty-one minutes, and fifty-six seconds. That means Rosie ran each mile in about five minutes for twenty-six miles straight. Yet she sprinted across the finish line with hardly a drop of sweat on her. How did she do it? The answer is that she cheated.

Rosie was born in Cuba in 1953. As an adult, she moved to Manhattan and became an administrative assistant for a company called Metal Trading Inc. In the fall of 1979 she applied to run the New York Marathon. She was late with her application, but the race officials let her in anyway because she said she was dying of brain cancer. She wasn't. She finished the New York race with a very respectable time of two hours and fifty-six minutes. She did so well that she came in twenty-third place and qualified for another race: the Boston Marathon.

The 1980 Boston race was one marathon fans were particularly excited about. A man named Bill Rodgers had won three years in a row, and fans were rooting for him to win a fourth time. Many spectators turned out to watch Bill run. Lots of those spectators had cameras because they were hoping to catch a glimpse of the first man ever to win the race four times in a row. He was a former Olympian who had been forced to quit because of a foot injury. Even with that injury, he was an impressive marathoner.

Bill did win the race, but his win turned out to be the least exciting thing about that day. What really stunned everyone — spectators and runners alike — was Rosie. Nobody knew who she was, yet she came in first with a time much improved from her New York run. A Canadian woman named Jacqueline Gareau was expected to win, but she came in second. What's more, Rosie stunned everyone by setting a record with the third

TWELVE BOSTON MARATHON FACTS

1. The marathon is held in April to commemorate Patriots' Day, a holiday celebrated only in Massachusetts and Maine.
2. The largest Boston Marathon was in 1996. More than 30,000 runners participated.
3. John A. Kelley has run the most times in the Boston Marathon. He's started in sixty-one races and finished fifty-eight times.
4. Bennett Beach has run the most Boston Marathons in a row. He's at forty-five straight years.
5. A half-million spectators come out to watch the race every year.
6. The race has raised more than $100,000,000 for charity.
7. In 2014 the oldest runner was eighty-one years old. The youngest was eighteen.
8. The Boston Marathon is the oldest continuously running marathon in existence. It started in 1897.
9. Women weren't allowed to run in the race until 1972.
10. Around 8,000 volunteers turn out to make sure the race goes smoothly.
11. The prize for winning the race is $150,000. You get an extra $25,000 if you set a record.
12. After crossing the finish line, runners are wrapped in Mylar blankets.

fastest time ever by a woman.

After the race, Bill and Rosie were awarded their medals and photographed. In the photo, Rosie smiles coyly with her laurel crown on her short-haired head. Her arm is raised above her head in triumph locked with Bill's hand in a sign of victory.

Trouble was brewing, though. Not three hours after the photography session, the race director announced that there was a problem. Nobody had seen Rosie at key checkpoint locations, nor was she visible at the starting point. Nobody could produce a picture of her. And remember that large crowds had turned up for this race, so it was strange that nobody could remember having seen her.

Rosie immediately became defensive when questioned. She said, "I ran the race. I really did." She even agreed to take a lie detector test. When questioned about how she improved by twenty-five minutes since New York, she couldn't answer with specific information about her training, nor could she explain why she wasn't very sweaty. All she could do was insist that she had run the race and that she had won. (You'd think she would have at least mussed her hair.)

Before long, witnesses came forward. Two college students from Harvard, John Faulkner and Sola Mahoney, had come to watch the race. It was a lovely spring day in the high sixties, and they wanted to soak up some sun and watch the runners while taking a break from their studies. Standing on the sidelines about a half mile from the finish line, John and Sola saw a woman enter the race from the crowd. They thought it was a joke. She didn't look like a runner, so they thought maybe she was just trying to fight the crowd. Or maybe she was just a joker. The next day, they saw a newspaper with Rosie's champion picture. They realized she was the woman who had entered the race right in front of them. They called the *Boston Globe* to report what they saw.

Race officials determined that Rosie could not possibly have run the race without being seen at one of the many checkpoints. With John and Sola's information, Rosie was sunk. She was stripped of her laurels and her medal. Jacqueline was crowned the official winner seven days after the race. She, in fact, set the record for third fastest women's time. Still, poor Jacqueline never got as much attention as Rosie did.

MARATHON HISTORY

The word *marathon* comes from the Greeks, but it probably doesn't mean what you think it does. It actually comes from the word that means "fennel," an herb.

In the fifth century, the Greeks and the Persians were fighting a war in a big field of fennel. As the story goes, the Greeks sent a guy named Phidippides to Sparta to get more men. Phidippides allegedly ran 150 miles in just two days, but it wasn't in enough time to send the men back to help the Greeks.

Even without extra men, the Greeks won the war and sent poor Phidippides running again. He ran from Marathon to Athens, a twenty-five-mile distance, to announce the victory.

The first commemorative marathon event happened more than a thousand years later, in 1898. Runners followed the path from Marathon to Athens to commemorate Phidippides' feat. The winner, Spyridon Louis, stopped for a glass of wine along the way and still won.

Later the marathon distance was set at 26.2 miles.

After the Boston debacle, a freelance photographer in New York came forward and said that Rosie had cheated there too. Rosie apparently started the New York Marathon, but then hopped on the subway. She rode for sixteen miles before getting out and walking across the finish line. The photographer on the train recalled speaking with Rosie because Rosie had said she sprained her ankle during the race and could not finish.

There was so much evidence against Rosie that you might think she would admit her lies and ask for forgiveness. She hasn't done either. She even insisted to Jacqueline that she had actually won the race. You have to wonder if Rosie is just a really persistent liar or if she truly believes she won the race.

Rosie is still alive today, but she has had other rough spots in her life. In 1982 she was accused of embezzling money from her workplace. She moved to Florida where she was arrested for conspiring to sell cocaine to undercover cops. She's now in her sixties, living in Florida, all the while insisting that she won the Boston Marathon.

I guess we have to give her credit for sticking with her story! •

LANCE ARMSTRONG

DATE: 1998–2013
THE LIE: That he wasn't using performance-enhancing drugs
REASON: Because using drugs is illegal

What's the longest you've ever ridden your bike? Well, if you were in the Tour de France, you'd ride 2,200 miles in twenty-three days. That's more than ninety-five miles a day! (Look at it this way: If you had to drive ninety-five miles, it would take you a little over an hour if you were going sixty-five miles per hour.)

Lance Armstrong won the Tour de France seven times, and the world was in awe of his strength and determination. He was an American sports hero.

Lance might have gone down in history as the world's greatest cyclist except for one important detail: He was taking performance-enhancing drugs for most of his career. Not only that, he had been vehemently denying it for ten years, lashing out against anyone who accused him of doping, a term that means taking performance enhancers.

In 2013 Lance admitted to Oprah that he had been doping for years. In just one day, he lost more than $1,000,000 in endorsements. He was stripped of his Tour de France medals and his Olympic medal. Worst of all for him, he was forbidden to participate in any competitive sport ever again.

It's true that Lance is a liar and a cheater, but the sport itself is as much to blame as he is. You see, competitive cycling has a long history of drug use. It was expected that anyone participating would take whatever performance-enhancing drugs he could. In the 1920s cyclers used cocaine. In the 1940s they used amphetamines. In 1963 fourteen cyclists had to drop out from morphine sickness. Between 1987 and 1992, at least twenty-three Tour de France competitors have died from using EPO, the blood-oxygen booster that Lance was in using. In 1997 seven teams — *entire* teams — were disqualified for using EPO.

Lance was far from the only person using EPO. He was simply the scapegoat, the person who got caught and used to issue an example to the sports world. In fact, a number of other doping cyclists testified against Lance. They only received a six-month ban as opposed to his lifetime ban.

So why did Lance take the fall when the sport itself is loaded with dopers? Well, there are a couple of reasons. First, Lance was a high-profile person. Not only had he dominated the sport of competitive cycling, but he was well known for his battle against cancer. When he was diagnosed in 1996, doctors told him he had no hope. But he survived and then went on to be one of the most famous athletes in all of history. His Lance Armstrong Foundation raised millions of dollars for cancer research.

But there's another reason that Lance had a target on him: Some people thought he was sort of a jerk. He's sometimes described as an outspoken control freak. He's been characterized as abrasive, narcissistic, and unable to hold his tongue. He's also incredibly impatient. In his younger days, his nickname was FedEx because he wanted everything overnight. He's been accused of pressuring his teammates to dope by threatening or intimidating them. When people close to him came forward and said they knew Lance was doping, he allegedly sued them or harassed them for speaking against him. In other words, he hasn't always been a pleasant person to be around.

Prior to his doping admission, at the height of his career, he was on top of the world. He dated Sheryl Crowe, a famous singer, and then Kate Hudson, a famous actress. He had million-dollar endorsements with Nike, which supported him for years when he was accused of doping. Nike was so sure he was clean that in 2004 they ran an ad where Lance explains in a voiceover that he's successful because he's on his bike "busting my a** six hours a day," not because he's doing drugs.

Trek Bicycle loved him because they sold twice as many bikes once Lance started shilling for them. The Lance Armstrong Foundation was bringing in millions of dollars in donations for cancer research. The foundation sold 90,000,000 Livestrong bracelets at a dollar a pop. (Do the math: That's

TOUR DE SALES

The Tour de France started as a way to sell more products. Can you guess which product? If you guessed bicycles, you are wrong. The race started as a publicity stunt to sell more newspapers.

NINE LANCE FACTS

1. In 2008 *Time* named him one of the 100 Most Influential People of the year.
2. He won his first triathlon when he was just thirteen years old.
3. He grew up in Plano, Texas.
4. He got his first bicycle when he was seven years old.
5. He moved to Colorado when he was a senior in high school to train for the Olympics.
6. When he was a kid, he used to ride his bike to Oklahoma. His mom would come pick him up.
7. He has three kids — twin daughters and a son.
8. He finished last in his first professional race.
9. He was tested for drugs twenty-four times in just one year.

$90,000,000 for cancer research.) Things were good for Lance.

In 2009 Lance's lies came back to haunt him in a big way. He'd won his last race in 2005, and if he'd stayed retired, he probably never would have been caught. But he wanted to ride again. The doping issue was getting a lot of attention at that time, so Lance went in clean. He really had no choice. Testing methods had gotten better. (They are so good now that they are basically foolproof.) He outperformed almost everyone even when he was clean.

But people wouldn't let up about how Lance won those races in the earlier part of his career. So many people knew he'd been doping during his earlier career that he was forced to admit it. He chose to confess to Oprah and the rest of the world because he wanted people to know that he took drugs before, but his 2009 win was totally clean.

His confession was not met with much sympathy. Not only was he stripped of his Tour de France titles, but he also lost his 2000 Olympic medal. He can't even participate in local swim meets in Austin, Texas, where he lives now. (That does seem a little extreme.) He was kicked out of the Lance Armstrong Foundation, even after giving $8,000,000 of his own money to them. They changed the foundation name to Livestrong, essentially wiping his name from the organization altogether. He lost his sponsors. He also lost a suit to SCA Promotions, his former promoters, and has to pay out $10,000,000 to them.

Lance has apologized for lying and harassing people, but he is clear that doping was basically required for the sport at the time. He didn't see it as cheating. "I viewed it as a level playing field," he once said. None of that mattered to the world, though. Lance's reputation was forever and irreparably harmed by lying.

In spite of his career-ending lies, Lance is doing his best to rebuild his life and his reputation. He lives in large house with an art collection, a wine cellar, and a pool. He hangs out there with his girlfriend and his children. He plays golf almost every day. He still reaches out to people who are suffering from cancer and encourages them to keep fighting. He'd like to go back to Livestrong, something that could happen in the future.

Most of all, he'd love to write a third book where he tells the truth about what happened. This time, he vows to tell the whole truth. •

SECTION 4:

ALIENS, GHOSTS, & CREATURE HOAXES

When I was a kid, I used to rush home from school every day to watch reruns of *The Brady Bunch*. One of my favorite episodes is the one where the boys try to scare the girls by playing a series of ghostly pranks on them. The prank war ends when their housekeeper, Alice, enters the house in the dark, sees the ridiculous bronze bust Mrs. Brady has made in homage to Mr. Brady, and swats the thing with her purse and smashes it to pieces. The kids lose their allowance for two weeks. Bummer.

That episode inspired hours of winter fun at my house. My brother and I would take turns "haunting" the basement while the other waited patiently upstairs. Then, when summoned, the upstairs dweller would tour the now-haunted basement. You lost if you got so scared you had to go upstairs. (We sound like imaginative kids, right? Not really. We called this game "Scare.")

Everyone likes a good scare now and then, but the difference between all-in-good-fun scaring and out-and-out hoax scaring is huge.

Before you get started reading this section, take the following quiz to see if your haunted pranks are all in good fun, the stuff of a good-natured game of "Scare," or if you are a full-on supernatural hoax-ster with questionable judgment, morals, or both.

ARE YOU A SUPERNATURAL LIAR?

Answer the following questions with "yes" or "no."

1. Have you ever painted a sheet blue and strung yourself up with Christmas lights to convince motorists that you are a little blue man from space?
2. Have you ever gone out to a wheat field late at night to flatten the crop in weird shapes and then claimed an alien did it?
3. Have you ever created a rubber dummy, filled the dummy with sheep guts, sewed it up, and then cut it open and pretended you just did an alien autopsy?
4. Have you ever carved a three-ton statue and then buried it behind your barn and pretended it was a prehistoric giant?
5. Have you ever mounted a plastic head on a toy submarine and then claimed you saw a mythical sea monster?
6. Have you ever disappeared for a few days only to return and say you'd been kidnapped and forced into marriage by a giant hairy beast?
7. Have you ever made paper doll fairies, photographed them, and then claimed that they were real and frolicking in the garden with you?
8. Have you ever visited a very famous castle in France and later told everyone you accidentally walked into the memory of a woman who had been dead for more than 300 years?
9. Have you ever made a documentary about a haunted house that was really just a regular house?

If you answered **no** to all of these questions, congratulate yourself. You might enjoy a rousing game of "Scare" every now and then, but you aren't trying to convince the world that a giant sea beast is living in the local lake or that you regularly picnic with fairies.

If you answered **yes** to any of these questions, you might want to rethink your life. You don't want to end up like those Brady kids. •

CHAPTER 12:
LITTLE SPACE PEOPLE

DON WEISS, LEROY SCHULTZ, & JERRY SPRAGUE

DATE: Spring 1958
THE LIE: Jerry was a little blue alien on the loose
REASON: Because they didn't have anything better to do

Have you ever hung out with your friends and come up with a brilliant idea for the best practical joke ever? That's exactly what happened to **Don Weiss**, **LeRoy Schultz**, and **Jerry Sprague** one spring day in Elkton, Michigan, in 1958. They were longtime buddies who were just home from military service and hadn't found jobs yet. So what did three unemployed young adults do? They hung out and talked about aliens and flying saucers, of course!

UFOs and potential alien life forms were a popular topic at the time. In fact, there was a catchy song playing on the radio called "Little Blue Man," sung by a singer named Betty Johnson. The song is an annoying little ditty about a person who is being followed by a little blue man — some kind of alien, presumably — who just repeats "I wuv you!" over and over again in a whiny voice. The person in the song keeps trying to ditch the little blue man but can't seem to shake him. At the end of the song, the person pushes the little blue man off a rooftop. But wouldn't you know it, that annoying blue man comes back and says, "I don't wuv you anymore." (Keep in mind that 1958 was a simpler time. People were delighted by this song.)

Don and his friends wondered if they could get people to believe that a little blue man really existed. They went foraging through their garages and found a bunch of junk that they used to build a costume. They started with a pair of long underwear that belonged to Jerry. Since he was the only one who fit in them, he was nominated to play the little blue man. He wore heavy combat boots and thick gloves. They stuck a football helmet on him to make his head appear round. Then they tossed a bed sheet over the helmet and cut two eyeholes in it with a scissors. They painted the whole costume with blue paint. It was a delightful surprise to discover that the paint seemed to glow in the dark.

The alien looked pretty convincing by this point, but the boys wanted to add one more detail: flashing lights. Something like that would be easy now. You'd just go to Target and buy a string of lights and a really long extension cord. But in 1958, flashing lights weren't something you could buy. So Don and his friends had to rig up something themselves. They created a battery-operated string of lights that they could wrap around their blue man creation. With his costume complete, Jerry looked like something from another planet. The boys were pretty pleased with their work. Now it was time to take their creation out in public.

The boys decided to be subtle. They didn't want their blue man jumping in front of cars or walking up to people and yelling boo. That was too obvious. Instead, they wanted people to see the alien creation from a distance. A fleeting glance of a little blue man is way scarier than a full-on look. Besides, if people got too close, they might figure out that the alien was just a kid in long underwear with a sheet over his head.

On a Thursday night, the boys decided they were ready to play their brilliant prank. Jerry got in the trunk of their car, and the boys drove out on a country road, parked out of sight from the road, and waited for cars

BARNEY AND BETTY HILL

On September 19, 1961, Barney and Betty Hill were driving back to their home in New Hampshire after a trip to Canada. From the car, they saw a UFO. They described it as a giant ship shaped like a cigar (paging Dr. Freud). They got out to investigate and claimed they saw nonhuman passengers. They were so scared, they ran back to the car.

Here's where the story gets really weird: They claimed they woke up two hours later with little memory of what happened. They were more than thirty miles from where they last remembered being. They both had memories of being given physical exams by small, gray aliens.

The reality is that Betty had read a book about UFOs around the time of this supposed event. She underwent hypnosis, convinced herself of the alien story, and then convinced Barney he saw the same things she did.

Old Barney loved Betty so much that he even participated in Betty's paranoid fantasies. Talk about true love.

ALIEN ABDUCTION

Ever wonder why people who claim they've been abducted by aliens tell such similar stories? That's because they've all seen the same media.

Take Betty Hill, for example. She claimed her abduction involved aliens sticking needles in her belly button. Just two weeks before Betty's alleged abduction, an episode of the popular show *The Outer Limits* told a story that included — what? You guessed it. An alien abduction with belly button needles.

The Outer Limits writers must have been taking it easy that week. That same storyline happened in *Buck Rogers in the 25th Century*. And that aired in 1930, thirty-one years before *The Outer Limits* episode.

to pass. Once they saw headlights coming, the boys signaled Jerry, who got out of the car and ran a few feet alongside the road. Then Jerry veered off the road and disappeared. In reality, he just ran back to his friends' car and got back into the trunk.

At first nobody seemed to notice that they were seeing a blue alien. The boys were persistent, though. They kept going out every Thursday night for about eight or ten weeks. Their hard work paid off after two months. Passersby started reporting sightings of a little blue man. Within a short period of time, it seemed like everyone in town was talking about the alien on the loose.

What amused the boys the most was the wildly different descriptions people were providing. Some people swore the alien was two feet tall. Another person said the alien was at least ten feet tall. One person said the alien ran faster than humanly possible. This bystander was convinced that the blue man had to be from some other planet. What else could explain his superhuman running? One motorist swore up and down that he saw the blue alien perched atop a telephone pole. (One wonders if this motorist should have been driving.)

The rumors seemed to get bigger and bigger the longer people talked about the little blue man. Everybody wanted to get a look at it. Some drivers got out of their cars to investigate for themselves, but Jerry always made sure to stay far away and run for cover as soon as someone started to chase him. It couldn't have been easy to run covered by a sheet and strung with Christmas lights, but Jerry did it.

The alien craze was great fun for the boys, but they eventually took things one step too far. One Thursday night, they saw a school bus approaching.

HISTORICAL HYSTERIA

Shared delusions are nothing new. In medieval times, a group of nuns believed they'd been attacked by devils. They convinced each other that they'd all experienced the same thing.

Even before that, a thousand years ago, some Greek women believed they had experienced, ahem, romantic relationships with animals. Again, they all reported similar experiences, but there was no evidence that they ever happened. (There's some evidence I wouldn't want to see.)

The bus was filled with junior high kids returning from a roller-skating party. Imagine those kids' surprise when they saw Jerry in his full costume running alongside the bus. Genuinely scared, the kids told their parents what they saw, and somebody called the police. The police headed out to the road and found Jerry and his friends parked in their car, waiting for their next mark to come along.

You might think the police would be angry. After all, they'd been fielding calls about the alien sighting for a few weeks, and they were surely tired of investigating the crazy claims people were making. But they thought the prank was funny. They laughed and even took a photo alongside Jerry dressed in his alien costume. That photo appeared in multiple publications, and the AP even picked up the story nationally. *Life Magazine* also ran the story and photo. The boys were famous!

The police knew that the boys couldn't keep pulling this hoax, though. Sooner or later, somebody was going to get hurt. So the officers told the boys to "take your underwear and go home." That's exactly what they did, but they didn't get rid of the costume. The football helmet is still on display in Don's barbershop in Elkton, Michigan. And if you Google Jerry's name, you'll find the famous photograph that millions of people were talking about way back in 1958.

You'd think their admission that they were pulling a prank would convince everyone in no uncertain terms that the little blue man was nothing more than a kid in long underwear. Not so. Some people still believe that they saw an alien, even after hearing Don and the boys confess.

Some people just want to believe. In their minds, little blue men are running around somewhere out there. We just have to wait until we are lucky enough to see one. •

DOUG BOWER & DAVE CHORLEY

DATE: 1978–1991
THE LIE: That aliens were making crop circles
REASON: Because they wanted to prove crop circle believers were nuts

---

In the 1970s, a strange phenomenon started happening: Patterns in crops of wheat, barley, and oats were appearing in farmland all over rural England. These designs — known as crop circles because they were usually round — seemed to show up overnight. Nobody could explain where they were coming from. Nobody but self-proclaimed cereologists, better known as crop circle believers. (Sometimes they are called croppies.) Crop circle enthusiasm in the '70s led to what is now known as circle mania.

Cereologists named themselves after Ceres, the Roman goddess of vegetation. (When you think about, that seems like a pretty boring thing to be a goddess of, but somebody had to do it.) Croppies believed (and still do) that the crop circles must have been coming from aliens. They just couldn't think of any other explanation. Sounds kind of wacky, right? I mean, I can think of about ten other explanations right off the top of my head, and none involve aliens. But the croppies were convinced.

Croppies were not totally sure what the circles represented, but they had some ideas. Here's what they posited.

1. The circles might be alien landing sites, or "UFO nests." That would make sense if alien ships are perfectly round, land in crops in the middle of the night, and then fly away before morning.
2. The circles might be evidence of paranormal energy. According to this theory, the circles were a supernatural side effect of aliens running around giving off all their otherworldly energy.

3. The circles might be small black holes. If you think black holes can only be in the sky, you'd be wrong, according to croppies.
4. The circles might be a communication device. This explanation was the most popular among circle-mania people. They believed that the circles were designed to send some kind of message, either to us or to each other.
5. The circles might be some kind of *Stargate*-esque gateway. Croppies who subscribe to this belief think that the crop circles might be a portal to some other locale.

None of these hypotheses are provable, but that hasn't stopped croppies from speculating. And there has been much to speculate about in the last forty years or so. Every summer, in some locale on earth, crop circles appear, and they are often impressive in size and complexity. Some are complicated pictograms or messages in English. No longer just a phenomenon in England, crop circles have turned up in the United States, Canada, China, Russia, Australia, and South Africa.

All this circle mania gave two men an idea: **Doug Bower** and **Dave Chorley** decided to make crop circles themselves. Armed with a plank tied to ropes, Doug and Dave stealthily flattened patterns in fields across England. A famous cereologist named Pat Delgado declared their crop circles to be absolutely the real deal. In fact, Pat definitively stated that no human could ever have done this work. (Pat was pretty sure of himself. He said there wasn't even a possibility that these circles were not alien in nature. That's a pretty big claim to stand behind.)

Imagine how excited Doug and Dave were when, years later, they revealed the truth about their handiwork. They were particularly gleeful when they showed Pat exactly how they made their crop circles, and he just looked like a fool.

That should have been the end of crop circle mania, right? Nope. Pat, the cereologist, said that while Doug and Dave might have made *some* of the crop circles, they could not have made *all* the crop circles. (Well, duh. But other people could have.) Pat maintained that real crop circles still existed, and those were created by "superior intelligence." He did admit, however, that Doug and Dave were pretty "fit" for a pair of men in their sixties.

Doug and Dave might have been pulling a hoax, but they went to great lengths to keep it a secret. For years, even their wives didn't know they were responsible for the crop circles popping up around England, so it was no wonder that croppies like Pat didn't believe them when they finally came clean. Here were two old men who admitted to making 200 "pictures," most of them appearing in Wiltshire County, home to Stonehenge, over the course of twenty years.

When Doug and Dave admitted their handiwork, some people did believe them. They even became sort of famous. They went on *Good Morning America* in 1991 to show how they made crop circles. It turns out that crop art is pretty easy if you can lift the tools and work at night with nothing but a flashlight attached to a hat. And you have to be willing to work nights.

Dave and Doug, along with other skeptics, tried to reason with croppies like Pat. They provided a list of evidence that strongly suggests all crop circles are manmade:

1. As media coverage of crop circles grew, more crop circles began appearing. The years 1981 to 1987 were ripe with media stories, and that's precisely when more crop circles started showing up. It's hard to believe that aliens are so attuned to our news that they decided to make more circles the more we talked about them.

2. Crop circles started in one relatively small area in England but spread to dozens of other areas all over the world as the media coverage grew. It seems strange that aliens would start in England and then begin moving to other countries just as the news reports arrived in those places.

3. Crop art became increasingly more complex as time went on. One message even read WEARENOTALONE. Perhaps aliens got better at their messaging, but it seems more likely that human pranksters got better at their hoaxes.

4. Crop circles always happened in private. When fields were put under camera surveillance, no crop circles would appear. Instead,

HOLLYWOOD CROP CIRCLES

Hollywood liked the idea of crop circles so much that filmmakers made a movie about them. *Signs*, released in 2002, stars Mel Gibson as a father who must protect his family from the aliens who are using his fields as their very own graffiti canvas. The crop circles in the movie are real, not a prank done by a couple of senior citizens.

CROP ART

Some crop graffiti is so beautiful that you'll agree it's a work of art. One of the biggest and most intricate works of crop art ever created is the Butterfly Human. It appeared in the Netherlands in August of 2009. The piece features a human in the middle with butterfly wings at his side. It seems to be making a comment about the evolution of humans.

Butterflies are popular objects for crop art. At least two other butterfly creations have been reported.

they'd appear in a field a few miles over. I suppose it's possible that aliens are just shy, but it seems strange that they would work for years undercover without ever giving themselves away.

Doug and Dave had pretty good points, but they inadvertently wound up contributing to the crop circle craze. In 1989 there were 250 reported crop circles. Just one year later, there were 700 instances of crop circles. Even today, at least three or four groups continue to do crop art. They call themselves "cereal artists." And the crop art they are making is certainly worthy of the moniker "art." In 2001 cereal artists made a design that was 800 feet across and contained more than 400 intertwined circles.

Sometimes crop circles are easily explained in other, much simpler ways. For example, croppies spotted what they believed to be crop circles in 2002 in Saskatchewan, Canada. The crop circles were actually piles of manure put there by a farmer cleaning out his barn.

Croppies are a dedicated group, though. They still believe that some crop circles are certainly "agrarian graffiti" done by tricksters like Doug and Dave, but they maintain that the aliens are alive and well and sending messages via wheat every chance they get. There's even a journal out there called *The Cereologist* to document and theorize about crop circles.

As for the farmers, you might wonder if they get annoyed waking up to find their grain fields flattened. Some might be ticked off, but one enterprising farmer turned his crop circles to his advantage. With farmland just a few miles from Stonehenge, this farmer set up a booth and charged a fee to tourists to see his crop circles. He made almost $50,000 in one month. What do you suppose the value of the crop was? If you guessed a whole lot less, you are right. The crop was worth $235. Nice work if you can get it! •

RAY SANTILLI

DATE: 1995

THE LIE: That he bought an authentic video of an alien autopsy

REASON: Because he wanted high ratings for his TV show

In 1947, in a tiny town in New Mexico called Roswell, an aircraft crashed. The U.S. government stated that the craft was a spy balloon, part of something called Project Mogul. The military wanted to use the balloon to monitor emissions from the supposed nuclear testing the Soviets were doing. Many conspiracy theorists, however, believe the government covered up an alien visit. One person, **Ray Santilli**, decided to capitalize on this belief.

For years, conspiracy theorists floated the rumor that the spy balloon story was a government cover-up. These theorists maintained that the ship was definitely alien in nature and that the U.S. government wanted to keep the rest of us from knowing that. Believers even argued that the government hid the wreckage and the alien passenger bodies at Wright-Patterson Air Force Base (east of Dayton, Ohio) in Hangar 18. That's oddly specific information, I know. The specifics just made the story feel more believable though. As the theory goes, the government secretly performed autopsies on the dead aliens as a means of studying their guts.

All this speculation about secret autopsies gave Ray an idea. Ray was (and actually still is) a music and video producer. Born in 1957 in England, he went on to found a company called AMP Management. He produced a number of popular new wave acts in the '80s. His client list included Boy George, Howard Jones, and the Thompson Twins. Aliens seem like a far cry from Boy George, but Ray knew an alien film would be ratings gold.

In 1995 Ray claimed that he had gotten hold of a secret military film. He said he bought twenty-two reels of film from a military cameraman who was present in 1947 when the U.S. government performed an autopsy on an alien body from the crashed ship. The military man claimed that he had stolen a copy of the film. Ray said he paid the man $100,000 for the reels.

On August 28, 1995, the Fox network aired that secret film on a TV special called *Alien Autopsy: Fact or Fiction?* The show was hosted by Jonathan Frakes, a star on *Star Trek: The Next Generation.* Not surprisingly, the show netted huge ratings for the network.

The secret military film footage was in black and white and was clearly shot with a shaky handheld camera. Fox viewers were able to see a female alien spread on a table. She was naked with no hair. Surgeons wearing biohazard suits stood over her and extracted organs. The camera captured some of the alien's oddities, including her twelve toes. Ray even inserted narrated footage of him buying the reels from the military man, now in his eighties. Many viewers were convinced that Ray had uncovered, once and for all, evidence that the U.S. government had been hiding evidence of alien life for years.

But not all viewers consumed what Ray was serving. Even some UFOlogists questioned the veracity of Ray's film. Astute viewers pointed out problems with the film. First, the alien's injuries were not consistent with a crash. You would expect that a body recovered from an air crash would be a little worse for wear. Not so in this case. This alien was in one piece with no marks or other visible injuries. Second, the surgeons performing the autopsy were holding the instruments wrong. Viewers who were medical professionals pointed out that surgeons are told to grasp a scissors in a particular way to hold it steady. The surgeons in the film held the scissors like the rest of us do. Other medical professionals pointed out that the alien body appeared to be made of rubber because it bounced when touched. They also noted that a thorough autopsy of this nature might take weeks. The surgeons in this film took just two hours. Finally, military experts pointed out that the military code marks shown in the film were obviously faked.

COPY CAT AUTOPSIES

Americans aren't the only people to believe our government is conducting secret autopsies on alien corpses. The Russians have their own story. Believers of that story maintain that a UFO crashed on Soviet soil in 1969. After the Russian military found the crash site and wreckage, they pulled out alien bodies and conducted autopsies. The details of this tale are almost exactly the same as the Roswell crash story.

Viewers identified so many holes in the story that Ray was forced to admit that the whole thing was a hoax, although he waited eleven years to come forward with the truth. In 2006 he told the world that the autopsy film was shot in an apartment. The alien body was created out of a synthetic material by a sculptor named John Humphreys. (John also played one of the surgeons in the film, proving himself to be a jack of all trades.)

Ray and John had used real body parts to extract from the fake body. The alien brain, for example, was actually a sheep's brain swimming in raspberry jam. The guts were bloody chicken entrails. Ray ensured that the camera never got too close to the body. When he did shoot a close-up, he made sure the camera was just a little bit out of focus. Even the most discerning viewers wouldn't be able to tell if they were seeing blood or jam. Ray intercut the faked autopsy footage with shots of alleged artifacts from the ship. He admitted he made the "artifacts" based on his imagination.

But what about the footage of Ray buying the reels from the military cameraman? Well, that was faked too. Ray paid a homeless man in his eighties to appear on film giving Ray the reels. That was actually shot in a cheap Los Angeles motel room.

To dispose of the faked evidence, Ray and John cut up the alien body parts and disposed of them in various garbage bins all over London. They knew nobody would be able to find enough pieces to put them all together and prove that the alien body was no more than a Hollywood prop.

Well, that settles it. Alien autopsy case closed.

Nope. Not quite.

Ray admitted he lied, but he claimed that the real footage does actually exist. He said that after he bought the reels, he realized they were too degraded to use. (You would think he would have checked that out before dropping a hundred large!) And even though he fully admitted to faking everything in the documentary, he maintained that the film is still real enough. He called it "a restoration."

Ray said he intercut a couple of frames from the real film, though he wouldn't identify which ones. When pressed, Ray couldn't come up with even a shred of evidence that the original reels ever existed. Ray maintains to this day that even though he lied and created an elaborate fake alien body, the real film does exist and he has it.

Conspiracy theorists maintain that even Ray's partial admission of guilt is itself a lie! They think the U.S. government forced Ray to say he faked everything in order to cover up the real autopsy. How's that for confusing? They think Ray's lie was a lie to cover up a government lie. It makes my head hurt just thinking about it.

You might think Ray blew his entire career with this stunt. Not so. He continues to be a successful music producer. In 2012 he produced a very successful film biography of a pop music group.

That group?

One Direction. •

CHAPTER 13:
SCARY CREATURES

THE LIAR:
GEORGE HULL

DATE: 1869

THE LIE: That his distant relative found a petrified giant buried behind his barn

REASON: Because he wanted to make biblical literalists look silly

---

We've all been in heated arguments before, but the difference between us and a guy named **George Hull** is that we didn't spend almost $3,000 to pull a prank involving five tons of gypsum in the late 1860s

George was a cigar maker by trade who lived in Binghamton, New York. He was also an atheist who liked to argue with religious people, especially those who believed the Bible was meant to be interpreted literally. While on business in Iowa, George began a heated argument with a Methodist preacher who was convinced that everything in the Bible was literally true. The preacher was particularly impressed by a line in Genesis that says giant men once roamed the earth. George couldn't convince him that such a statement could not be proven, but he came up with an idea instead, one that could earn him a little money and make people like the preacher look foolish. He decided he would create a fossil of a giant man.

George began working on his scam almost immediately. He ordered the five tons gypsum from Fort Dodge, Iowa. It cost $2,600, which was a fair amount of money back in the late 1800s. (Frankly, it's a fair amount of money now. Can you imagine spending two grand to pull a prank?) George knew his purchase might raise some eyebrows, so he covered his tracks by saying he was planning to make a patriotic statue. That seemed to answer any questions the gypsum supplier might have had.

The block of material was sent to a stonecutter named Edward Burghardt who lived in Chicago. Edward carved a "fossil" designed to look like a petrified human giant. The giant was ten feet long and weighed 2,990 pounds. It had twenty-one-inch feet and shoulders that were three feet across. Even the statue's nose was huge. The nostrils were three feet across. (Measure your nostrils. I bet they aren't even an inch wide.) Edward shipped this masterpiece to Cardiff, New York — just a few miles from Syracuse.

The receiver of Edward's creation was William C. Newell, a farmer from Cardiff known by his friends and neighbors by the name of Stub. Stub was a distant relation of George, and he happened to have a farm where George could hide this giant fossil. Stub buried the statue behind his barn, and then he waited a year to hire some men to dig a well. His real goal was to get someone to find the carving, someone besides him. The discovery would be more believable that way. Imagine the workers' surprise when they uncovered that stone man, just as Stub and George had planned.

Stub — under the supervision of George — began charging people to see the fossil. People who believed it was a petrified man were delighted because the fossil seemed to prove the book of Genesis. These fossil enthusiasts were called "petrificationists." People who didn't believe it was a fossil still thought it was something important. Those people insisted it was a seventeenth-century statue carved by Jesuits to impress the Native Americans. (Where they found evidence for such a claim is a mystery.) Regardless of which position they believed, people were very interested in seeing this giant thing. They turned up in droves to Casa Stub.

One of those visitors was Andrew Dickson White, co-founder of Cornell University. Andrew was amazed at how many people journeyed to Stub's place. At first glance, he thought it looked like "a county fair," but the crowds were quiet and reverent as they lined up to look at the giant housed in a tent. You had to get up pretty early in the morning to fool Andrew; he recognized immediately that this was a hoax. First, he noted that the statue could not be a fossil because he could clearly see the carving marks. Second, he knew it wasn't a religious symbol because it wasn't sculpted as an idol. Third, it was clear to him that the thing wasn't old. Remember that it had only been in the ground for a year, so it was practically brand new. Finally, Andrew questioned why the well diggers would have been digging in that particular place in the first place. It wasn't a convenient location for water, which led Andrew to believe that Stubs had planted the giant man there with the idea that he would have hundreds of people traipsing through to look at it. Andrew was appalled that people would so easily believe what was so clearly a fake.

But the general public was far more gullible than Andrew. They couldn't stop talking about the petrified man, or what they called the Cardiff Giant.

Stubs — with George still behind him calling all the shots — eventually sent the Cardiff Giant to Syracuse to be studied by a paleontologist named Othniel C. Marsh. Othniel was no dummy. Like Andrew, he took one look at it and declared it a hoax. People didn't care. In spite of Othniel's pronouncement, the petrificationists maintained that this was the real deal — proof that the Bible is literal. They believed the experts were just trying to cover up the truth. People from all over still lined up to see the giant, preferring to believe ordinary citizens over experts.

THE HISTORY OF A SUCKER

P.T. Barnum, the famous showman, is frequently credited with this famous line: "There's a sucker born every minute." But did you know he never said it?

The person who first said that line was one of the businessmen who bought the Cardiff Giant from Stub (via George Hull). The businessman said the now famous line when P.T. announced he was going to display his own fake Cardiff Giant. The businessman was criticizing the people who would pay to see P.T.'s fake of a fake.

That's pretty rich coming from someone who paid more than $30,000 for a few tons of gypsum.

The Cardiff Giant was such a draw that some businessmen offered to buy it from Stubs. In consultation with George, Stubs worked out a deal. The businessmen paid $37,500 for the thing. (Not bad for a couple thousand dollars of gypsum.) George was overjoyed. He'd not only tricked biblical literalists, but made some money too. Even better.

The businessmen displayed the Cardiff Giant in Syracuse where they charged a fee to see it. They were making so much money that they attracted the attention of a legendary showman by the name of P.T. Barnum. Clever P.T. offered them $60,000 to lease it for three months. He figured he could put it in his New York museum of oddities and cash in himself. The businessmen were greedy, though. They told him absolutely not. So P.T. commissioned his own Cardiff Giant to be made. That meant there were now two Cardiff Giants on display in New York! The businessmen tried to sue P.T., but a judge threw out the case. The original Cardiff Giant was a fake, so there was nothing stopping P.T. from making a fake of a fake. (P.T.'s version actually made more money.)

Eventually the excitement died down and people lost interest in the Cardiff Giant. The original, from Stub's farm, is now in a museum called the Farmers' Museum in Cooperstown, New York. (That's right down the road from the Baseball Hall of Fame.) The P.T. Barnum replica is in Detroit at a museum called Marvin's Marvelous Mechanical Museum.

People might not be interested in the Cardiff Giant anymore, and such a thing might not have attracted any attention at all, save for the fact that in the late 1800s science and religion were a hot topic. Many religious people

SIX THINGS YOU SHOULD
KNOW ABOUT CARDIFF, WALES

1. Cardiff is the capital of Wales.
2. The city began as a Roman fort.
3. Cardiff Castle has been around since the eleventh century.
4. The National History Museum is the most visited place in the city.
5. The population is just under 350,000 people.
6. Wales offers nightly family ghost walks. (I'm not sure if that means you and your family walk or if the ghost family does. Either way, it only costs five pounds.)

wanted to find ways to prove a scientific basis for religion. The Cardiff Giant capitalized on that desire. Even when experts definitively declared the carving a hoax, people wanted to believe. So they did. Because belief comes from a place that doesn't necessarily reside in the same brain space as logic. That doesn't make believing bad. It just means that people believe in things for all kinds of reasons that aren't necessarily rational.

Andrew was probably the most upset about the Cardiff Giant. He was terribly disappointed that the public was simply ignoring the evidence and George's eventual confession of his hoax. He wrote this line in his auto-biography: "At no period of my life have I ever been more discouraged as regards the possibility of making right reason prevail among men." Andrew was saying that he was disappointed that people didn't display much reasoning ability. He had more faith in people before the Cardiff Giant, but that carved statue proved that people believed what they wanted to believe, even if the belief defied reason.

If Andrew was disappointed in the public then, it's a good thing he died before the Kardashians got their reality shows. Then he *really* would have been discouraged about human potential. •

THE LIAR:

MARMADUKE WETHERELL

DATE: 1934

THE LIE: That a photo snapped by a surgeon was of the famed Loch Ness monster

REASON: Because he wanted to embarrass a British newspaper

The Scottish Highlands are perhaps most famously known for a body of water called the Loch Ness, a 788-foot-deep lake. For thousands of years, rumors have circulated that the water is home to a monster, a terrifying mythical creature that specializes in killing unsuspecting Loch Ness visitors. The story is so old that it dates back to the first century. When the Romans came to Scotland, they found tattooed tribes that they named the Picts, or painted people. The Picts drew pictures that the Romans didn't recognize. One appeared to be a monster with a beak, a spout, and flippers. It looked a little bit like a water elephant. That strange mythical beast became the first representation of the Loch Ness Monster, a giant, water-loving beast who possessed magical powers that lured people to their death.

The story morphed into all sorts of legends that spread through Scotland. In one of the stories, Saint Columba, the man credited for bringing Christianity to Scotland, allegedly saw the monster getting ready to attack a man. Saint Columba told the monster to leave. The monster — evidently quite a compliant beast — turned around and swam away. The imperiled man was saved.

Stories about the Loch Ness Monster continued for a thousand years, but they got really popular in the 1930s. That's when a road was built along the shoreline of the loch. For the first time in history, people could easily get to the water by automobile. Reports of the monster became increasingly frequent, so frequent that a circus offered 20,000 pounds for the monster's capture. In the 1930s alone, more than 4,000 people claimed to have seen the Loch Ness Monster with their own eyes, yet nobody had a single shred of proof.

A newspaper called the *Daily Mail* decided to hire someone to investigate one of these claims. A couple out for a pleasant day at the lake said they saw a monster in the water, a story that was reported in the *Inverness Courier*, another newspaper. The *Daily Mail* hired a game hunter and movie producer by the name of **Marmaduke Wetherall** to go check things out. (What a great name, right? He looked like a crazy old prospector from a black-and-white western movie.) Marmaduke found what he believed to be monster tracks leading into the loch. He was thrilled and immediately filed a report for the paper.

When experts from the Natural History Museum caught word about the alleged tracks, they came out to have a look for themselves. They figured out pretty quickly that there was a reasonable explanation: The tracks belonged to hippo feet, not a mythical sea beast.

I bet you didn't know there are hippos in Scotland. Well, there aren't. And there never were. These hippo tracks belonged to an umbrella stand. The fashion at the time was to use imported hippo feet as the base of these pieces of furniture. Some trickster had fooled Marmaduke. (And some poor hippo lost his feet in the service of umbrellas. Never buy an umbrella stand unless you first make sure no animals were harmed in the making of the product.)

The newspaper blamed Marmaduke, making him out to be a complete fool. Marmaduke was livid because he was suddenly a laughingstock all over Britain. First he got mad, and then he vowed to get even. He decided he was going to present the newspaper with a faked photograph, one so authentic looking that they would publish it. Then he would reveal his hoax, and the newspaper would be the dummy. Marmaduke reportedly said, "We'll give them their monster." (I imagine that this line was followed with an evil laugh.)

Marmaduke began his scheme by contacting his stepson, Christian Spurling, a model maker. Christian used a toy tin-plated submarine as a base and then attached a serpent-like head carved out of a type of plastic that looks like wood. The beast's head was only about a foot long, but Marmaduke knew someone could take a photo from a distance and then crop it to make the beast appear larger.

The only problem now was who was going to take the photo and present it to the press. It couldn't be Marmaduke because his reputation was in tatters. And it certainly couldn't be Christian because everyone would connect him to Marmaduke. So Marmaduke contacted a respected gynecologist named Robert Kenneth Wilson, an unassuming man with a neat mustache. People wouldn't question a doctor with nice facial hair.

In 1934 Robert shot a photo of the fake Loch Ness Monster, a photo that was then cropped by Marmaduke. The story Robert told the world went like this: He claimed that he had driven up to the loch to photograph birds. He saw something in the water, stopped his car, and got out to capture an image. He claimed that he didn't even believe in the Loch Ness Monster. But the photo had changed his mind. This was a brilliant addition to the story. People love when skeptics convert.

The world was fascinated by this photo, which was referred to as the "Surgeon's Photo." Even skeptics couldn't quite find a way to prove it was faked. They tried though. Some Loch Ness Monster doubters speculated that it was a bird or an otter. Believers scoffed at doubters and said the photo was finally definitive proof that some otherworldly creature was living in the deep waters. Cryptozoologists — people who study supernatural animals — used Marmaduke's picture to bolster their claims that something called a plesiosaur existed. The plesiosaur is a sort of dinosaur-fish hybrid that looked a lot like Nessie.

Not surprisingly, after the publication of the photo, more and more people started seeing the Loch Ness Monster (or believed they were seeing it). That's the funny thing about supernatural beings: The more we talk about them, the more people believe they've seen them. Soon everyone wanted to catch an eyeful of Nessie — and why not? Wouldn't you want to see a giant elephant-like sea beast who had the power to lure you into the sea and then eat you in one bite? (Hmm, on second thought, maybe you should just wait in the car.) Nevertheless, for sixty years, Loch Ness Monster hunters looked for the creature Robert photographed. Everybody wanted to get a second photo of it. Really ambitious Nessie hunters dreamed of capturing the great beast.

Then, in 1994, something surprising happened. Christian, ninety years old at the time, confessed that his stepfather, Marmaduke, orchestrated the hoax. He gave specific details about how he created the submarine with the carved serpent head. He was able to talk about what the photo looked like before it was cropped, something he would not have been able to do if he hadn't seen the original photo. Christian said that Marmaduke fully

THE OTHER MARMADUKE

The much more famous Marmaduke is not even human. He's a dog. A Great Dane, to be exact. He's the star of a comic strip drawn and written by Brad Anderson since 1954. It's about the Winslow family and their very large and friendly dog. Brad sold his first cartoon when he was still in high school. He made a cool three bucks. Now he's ninety years old and still drawing. In 2010 Hollywood released a movie version of the strip. Marmaduke was voiced by Owen Wilson. His love interest, a shepherd dog, was voiced by Emma Stone.

LOCH NESS MONSTER RIDES

The handiest way to get driving directions is with Google Maps. This convenient tool not only can tell you how long it will take you to catch a bus from Fort Augustus to Urquhart Castle in Scotland (thirty-two minutes), but will also tell you how long it will take via Loch Ness Monster. It's supposed to be a joke, but you have to wonder how many people think it proves Nessie is real.

Incidentally, it's four minutes faster to hop on the sea serpent than it is to take the bus. But the bus is probably drier. And safer.

intended to reveal the hoax to embarrass the *Daily Mail*, but the photo became so famous that he decided to let the hoax go on. Eventually he died and so did Robert, the respectable doctor. Christian was the only living person who knew about the scam, and he decided he wasn't going to carry this secret to his grave.

Many Nessie believers accused Christian of lying. They started looking for holes in his story. Some said the kind of toy submarine he claimed to have used didn't exist in 1934. It did, by the way. Others claimed that Christian was lying in order to sully Marmaduke's reputation, and since he was dead, he couldn't offer his side of the story. Christian, however, offered pretty convincing evidence that Marmaduke had cooked up the whole scam. Christian maintained his story until he died.

In spite of Christian's claim that he made the toy model and the fact that no 100 percent credible pictures of Nessie exist, some people still believe — wholeheartedly believe — there is such a monster. Some go to great lengths to prove it's out there. In 2003 a show on the British Broadcasting Corporation (BBC) used 600 sonar beams to track Nessie. Not surprisingly, they found nothing.

The search for Nessie continues. But I wouldn't recommend you hold your breath until it's found. You'd be better off making a model Nessie for your bathtub. •

BIGFOOT HUNTERS

DATE: 1950s–present
THE LIE: That they've seen and/or filmed a Bigfoot
REASON: Because they want people to believe Bigfoot exists

You might have noticed that a lot of cryptozoologists are obsessed with a creature called Bigfoot, also known as Sasquatch. Turn on your television and you'll find whole shows dedicated to hunting this creature. **Bigfoot hunters** are a dedicated group. No credible evidence exists for Bigfoot, yet enthusiasts keep searching, even when claim after claim turns out to be a blatant hoax.

The legend of Bigfoot has been around for hundreds of years, but the name Bigfoot didn't become popular until 1959. That's when an article published by Ivan T. Sanderson in *True Magazine* came out describing mysterious footprints in California. Eyewitnesses came forward and said they too had seen something resembling this Bigfoot creature. Nobody was able to present credible evidence, but the story stuck.

In 1967 Roger Patterson and Bob Gimlin shot a short film in Bluff Creek, California. That film showed an alleged lady Bigfoot walking through a forest clearing. Bigfoot enthusiasts believed for years that this film was the best evidence for Bigfoot in existence.

Unfortunately for believers, the film turned out to be a hoax. Years later, the people involved in the deception stepped forward with the truth. According to these folks, Roger, who died in 1972, came up with an idea for shooting a Bigfoot film, so he called up a married couple who made movie costumes. The couple created a hairy suit and sold it to Roger. They later confessed to their role in the hoax.

The next person to come forward was Clyde Reinke. He was a photographer for a movie company that made wildlife films. The movie company thought a Bigfoot short would be a nice palette cleanser between their more serious nature films. Clyde was hired to shoot the Bigfoot out and about in nature. He came clean years later.

The most damning evidence for the film as a hoax came from a guy named Bob Heironimus. He was twenty-six years old in 1967. Roger and Bob Gimlin approached him about wearing the Bigfoot suit for the film. Bob Heironimus was poor, so he agreed to do it for $1,000 and a cut of the film's profits. (Poor Bob never did get paid. He would have been better off getting a paper route.)

For the film, Bob donned the suit, which was made of fur and horse leather. It stunk, and he could barely see out of it. That's because the headpiece was a sort of football helmet covered with material. Bob only had two small eyeholes to see through. The suit was filled out with football pads, so it was very hot inside. Bob had a heck of a time trying to maneuver while wearing it. On top of that, he suffered from a little bit of claustrophobia. Still, he was able to wear the suit long enough to appear on film for a minute or so. When the shoot was over, Bob threw the suit in the trunk of his mom's car. He was probably grateful to be done with the thing.

Later, his mother found the suit in her car. She was understandably perplexed. She called up her sister-in-law, who lived down the street, and asked her to come have a look. Bob's nephew, who was eight at the time, recalled playing with the hairy costume while his mother and his aunt discussed what in the world Uncle Bob was up to. Bob himself was asleep in his bed, worn out from his Bigfoot appearance.

The fact that so many people saw the costume is important to this story. Why would so many people confess to a hoax? And how could they all know so many true details if they were lying? For instance, Uncle Bob knew things he could not have known had he not seen the suit. And his family corroborated his story, as did the costume makers and the filmmakers. Uncle Bob claimed his confession was motivated by nothing more than being tired of lying for thirty-seven years. It's understandable that he would get tired of never being able to tell his kids that he was once Bigfoot.

Roger and Bob's film might be one of the most famous Bigfoot hoaxes, but it's not the only one. In 1976 Cherie Darvell was on a Bigfoot hunt in Eureka, California, with a film crew. While on the hunt, she was kidnapped. The film crew caught an alleged Bigfoot snatching Cherie under his arm around 11 a.m. (The alleged film footage has never been released.) The crew claimed they lured Bigfoot by setting out marshmallows soaked in lady's pee and menstrual blood. The crew members said they were so surprised by Bigfoot kidnapping poor Cherie that they just froze and didn't even try to save her. They saw enough though to report that the monster had feet that were twenty inches long.

The county spent $11,613 looking for Cherie, probably assuming that the crew had taken her because they didn't believe all the Bigfoot jazz. A few days into the search, Cherie turned up on her own at a resort. She appeared just fine. She was not dirty and not hurt; rather, she smelled like a woman who had recently bathed. The Bigfoot hunters claimed that she was visibly shaken, beaten up, and holding her broken ribs, but no newspaper report verified that claim. They all said the opposite. Cherie herself said in an interview that she had been kidnapped by Bigfoot and taken as his bride. (That sounds pretty scary. Can you imagine having to marry a beast best known for being smelly?)

Cherie never admitted to lying, but her story is largely regarded as a hoax. Neither she nor the film crew was ever able to produce any evidence of her supposed kidnapping. If Bigfoot had taken a bride, wouldn't he come back for her? At the very least, wouldn't he try to kidnap another lady after the first one escaped?

Some Bigfoot spotters have admitted they are liars. In 1982 a man named Rant Mullens (with a name like that, Bigfoot Hunter is the only logical occupation) admitted that he'd been making fake tracks for years. Another liar, Tom Biscardi, said he captured a Bigfoot in 2005 that was eight feet tall and weighed 400 pounds. Tom was never able to produce the creature, which might be why he later admitted that the whole thing was a publicity stunt for a film he was making. In 2008 Matt Whitton and Rick Dyer claimed to have captured a Bigfoot in Georgia and put him in the freezer after taking DNA samples and photos. Later they admitted that the Bigfoot was just a costume made of rubber.

Bigfoot hoaxes might be all in good fun at times, but they can be deadly. In 2012 poor Randy Lee Tenley of Montana dressed in a hairy costume and

BIGFOOT RESEARCH

If you are interested in searching for the mystery man himself, you can join the BFRO, otherwise known as the Bigfoot Field Researchers Organization. It was founded in 1995 and remains the only Bigfoot research organization (that I know of). Pack your bags because the BFRO launches new expeditions all the time. Be sure to pack your wedding gown… just in case.

OCCAM'S RAZOR

Almost 700 years ago, a really smart guy named William of Ockham said something really important: "Plurality should not be posited without necessity." What he meant is that if you have more than one theory or explanation, the simpler one is the one you should go with. He apparently used this line of reasoning so often that it came to be known as Occam's Razor.

Let's try it out. Suppose I told you I found some fresh poop in the woods, which I picked up (ew, gross) and showed to you. The complicated theory is that the poop belongs to a mythical monster named Bigfoot. The simple theory is that it belongs to a bear. In which case, I'm lucky I got out of there alive!

ran along the side of a highway to incite Bigfoot reports. The stunt ended tragically when he was hit by a car and died.

Bigfoot believers admit that maybe some people lie, but, they argue, not everyone does. They think strong Bigfoot evidence exists. For example, they would ask how can you explain all the hair, blood, and poop samples they've produced over the years? I can answer that, actually. The reality is that the samples usually yield a reasonable explanation. Hair is often from bears or cows. Blood samples have ended up being nothing more than transmission fluids. And the poop belongs to any creature that poops in the woods, including humans. When DNA tests do prove inconclusive, that doesn't mean the samples *must* belong to Bigfoot. It just means that the samples are too degraded or that scientists don't have a DNA match on file. An inconclusive result means the DNA could just as easily belong to Santa Claus as Bigfoot. Believers would tell me I'm naive.

So why do people continue to believe in Bigfoot?

The answer is very simple: Because they (and maybe we) want to. •

CHAPTER 14:
BOO!
GHOSTS
& SPIRITS

FRANCES GRIFFITHS & ELSIE WRIGHT

DATE: 1917–1981

THE LIE: That they'd seen and photographed fairies

REASON: Because Frances needed a reason to explain why she fell into a pond

One pleasant summer day in 1917, two young cousins spent the afternoon playing in their garden in Cottingley, England. Their mothers warned them to avoid the beck (a small stream), but the girls were curious. While jumping across slippery stones, one of the girls, **Frances Griffiths**, fell in. She was completely soaked. Back at the house, she was forced to admit to her mother and her aunt that she'd disobeyed. Why, her mother wanted to know, was she playing near the water when she'd been specifically ordered to steer clear of it? Because, the little girl said, she was chasing fairies. Her mother accused her of lying and sent her off to change into dry clothes.

That little lie — that she'd chased fairies across the beck — seemed innocent enough, but it was a lie that would live on for more than sixty years! That's because Frances's older cousin, **Elsie Wright**, had an idea. She borrowed her father's camera in order to prove the fairies existed. They went back outside and shot pictures. Elsie begged her father to develop the photos right away. Sure enough, Arthur Wright discovered pictures of the girls cavorting with fairies. There was even a photo of one of the girls lounging with a gnome. Hogwash, Arthur, a skeptic, proclaimed! But Elsie and Frances took the camera out again and came back with more fairy photos. Instead of being impressed, Elsie's father was so fed up that he forbade them from using the camera again.

The photos might have been forgotten except for one thing: Elsie's mother, Polly Wright, believed in the supernatural. Two years after the pictures were taken. Polly attended a lecture on spiritualism. The specific topic was theosophy, or the study of nature spirits. After the lecture, she approached the speaker and told him she had fairy photos. The speaker was intrigued and asked to see those pictures. The photos ended up in the hands of a professional photographer named Harold Snelling. Harold examined them carefully and pronounced them 100 percent real. He declared that there was no possible way the pictures could have been falsified.

Not surprisingly, word got out that pictures of fairies existed. One famous person was eager to see them. That person was Sir Arthur Conan Doyle, author of the Sherlock Holmes stories. He, by coincidence, had just been commissioned by *Strand Magazine* to write an article about fairies. That article would come out in December of 1920. Perfect! He could include photos with his essay.

Soon after Sir Arthur's article was published, everyone was talking about the girls who had captured fairies on film. In 1921 a man named Geoffrey Hodson, an expert in spiritualism, came to see the fairies at the Wright home. He was a self-proclaimed clairvoyant, and he was very interested in the spirit world. He reassured the girls and their parents that he saw the fairies too. Another man, a spiritualist like Geoffrey, believed the fairies were a troupe of miniature dancers. How delightful!

The fact that an expert photographer (Harold), a famed writer (Sir Arthur), and a supposed expert (Geoffrey) all believed the photos to be authentic went a long way to convincing other people that the photos were real.

Here's the rub: They *were* real photos, but the fairies were as fake as Katy Perry's blue wig.

Elsie, the older girl, was a budding artist. She'd taken some classes at a nearby school and was known to sketch fairies in her sketchbooks. Frances, who had come from South Africa to live with the Wright family with her mother while her father was fighting in World War I, brought with her a book. That book was called *Princess Mary's Gift Book*, and it was published in 1915. The book was filled with pretty fairy drawings, drawings that Elsie perfectly copied on heavy paper. With her mother's tailoring scissors, she cut out the fairies. Together the girls used hat pins to fasten the fairies to the ground. Then they took the photos. After the photo session, they tossed the paper cuttings into the pond to be sure there was no evidence of the cutouts.

The photos themselves are fascinating. They are black and white, of course, and feature the girls posing with spritely but very tiny fairies. Both girls are angelic looking with long curls and friendly smiles. If you don't look too closely, the photos appear to be of two healthy and happy young girls on a bright summer's day hanging out with a pack of fairies.

Arthur Wright, who was no dummy, spotted the trick immediately. Why were there scraps of papers in the grass? The girls swore up and down that he was seeing things. There was no paper in the grass! He refused to believe their story; he wanted to put a stop to this whole ruse. But with Arthur Conan Doyle on their side, the girls were suddenly thrust into the limelight. Even if they had wanted to admit their scam, they didn't feel they could. They were forced to weave a grand story about their interaction with fairies. Frances even wrote letters home to her friends in South Africa about

SIX FAIRY TYPES

1. Brownies help around the house for small gifts and treats.
2. Hobgoblins are mischievous spirits who like to play tricks.
3. Banshees are female spirits who wail when someone is about to die.
4. Goblins are tiny little creatures who have magical abilities and are greedy.
5. Bug-a-boos are scary monsters, similar to the boogeyman.
6. Mermaids (and mermen) are underwater creatures who are half human and half fish.

the fairies she'd seen. She hypothesized that she never saw them back home because Africa was too hot.

Arthur Conan Doyle and the spiritualist community might have been firm believers, but many other people questioned the veracity of the fairies. These skeptics provided five very good reasons to doubt the reality of fairies.

1. The girls aren't looking at the fairies in the photos. That seems odd. If you saw a fairy, wouldn't you want to check it out pretty closely? The girls claimed they were just so used to them that they stopped looking at them.
2. Some of the fairies were missing wings. That seemed strange. Why would a one-winged fairy exist? Had it lost one in a freak accident? Was it a birth defect? Or did the girls simply forget to draw the second wing?
3. In one of the photos, Elsie's hand is super-long and distorted. She looks like a normal girl with an alien hand. The photo suggests that Frances was playing around with the camera to make the fairies look more lifelike. In doing so, Elsie's hand came out looking like it belonged to a giant.
4. The fairies are dressed in high-fashion French clothes. One looks like a flapper girl who just stepped out of a Parisian nightclub. It seems unlikely that fairies would be sporting the very same fashions shown in the latest magazines.
5. The most important clue, though, was that the fairies *looked* like paper cutouts. It's pretty hard to look at the photos and think, "Yup! That looks like a bunch of real live fairies and not like

cardboard figures pinned to the grass." To be fair, people weren't used to looking at photos, so it was probably easier to fool them with the slightest trick. You and I are so steeped in visual imagery that we can spot faked evidence a mile away. In 1920 many people had never even seen photographs before.

Lots of fairy enthusiasts didn't give two bits about any of the evidence suggesting the photos were scam. For example, when someone pointed out that you could see the black tip of a hat pin on the gnome's belly, Arthur Conan Doyle retorted that it was simply his belly button. Because gnomes have belly buttons, Arthur insisted.

There were other reasons people believed. World War I had just come to a close, and England was weary and beaten up by a war that destroyed many lives. The fairy story was a much-needed diversion. It was a welcome relief to the news they'd been hearing for years about death and destruction. People loved talking about Alice and Iris — those were the names Arthur Conan Doyle gave Frances and Elsie in his article — and their fairy friends. They were as famous as beloved TV stars now.

In 1966, forty-nine years later, the *Daily Express* interviewed Elsie. She intimated that she might have been pulling everyone's leg. She was later evasive when asked point blank if she had lied about the fairies. In 1978 James Randi, the famous magician and skeptic, got his hands on a copy of the fairy book that had inspired Elsie in the first place. That seemed to be pretty damning evidence against the girls.

A few years later, in 1981 and again in 1982, Elsie admitted that the photos were faked. She confessed and provided details of how they took the photos. Elsie was surprised that people believed them in the first place. Frances backed up Elsie's story, but maintained that the last photo was real.

In a surprising twist to the story, both Frances and Elsie claimed to have taken the last photo (neither girl was in the photo). On top of that, both women maintained that they really did see fairies, but they faked the pho-

THE MOVIE TREATMENT

The Cottingly fairy photos were ripe for a film treatment. In 1997 a movie with the unimaginative title of *Photographing Fairies* was released in the U.K. But the movie plot is markedly different (and far less interesting) than the real story.

FOUR FAMOUS FAIRIES

1. Black Annis — a hag fairy with a blue face
2. Gentle Annie — a kind fairy who governs storms
3. Will-o-the-wisp — a mean fairy who haunts bogs (tough gig)
4. Tooth Fairy — an overworked fairy who hoards human teeth (weird)

tos because they didn't think anybody would believe them. Keep in mind, Elsie also admitted they faked the photos to fool the adults and get Frances out of trouble for falling into the beck. So neither Frances nor Elsie has a great truth-telling track record.

It's more likely that Elsie and Frances convinced themselves they really saw fairies to justify the lie they held onto for sixty-plus years. Maybe after all those years, they even believed their lies themselves. Or maybe they were just too ashamed to admit how many people they fooled.

If fairies do exist, and they frolic in the garden, I recommend you walk softly. Those little things are fragile. •

ANNE MOBERLY & ELEANOR JOURDAIN

DATE: 1901–1937

THE LIE: That they'd entered the memories of Marie Antoinette

REASON: Because at least one of them believed they did

In 1901 **Anne Moberly** was the principal of the prestigious St. Hughes College at Oxford, England. Anne was considering hiring **Eleanor Jourdain**, the headmistress at an all-girls' school, to be the vice principal. Eleanor had a degree in history from Oxford, so her credentials were quite solid. But Anne wanted to be sure that they would work well together. They agreed to meet and vacation together in France where Eleanor was staying for the summer. Talk about an extended job interview!

One day the two ladies decided to tour the Palace of Versailles, just outside Paris. They toured the château itself but were largely unimpressed. (That tells you something about the two women right there. The palace is probably the most impressive castle in the world.)

Anne and Eleanor decided they'd wander the gardens to see what else might interest them. They settled on the Petit Trianon, a small castle on the grounds of Versailles. Unfortunately, they got lost searching for the structure, which is about a half mile from the main castle. While they were walking among the trees, paths, and streams, something weird happened: They were overcome with a strange feeling, one that they could only characterize as a sort of depression. As they walked around in this negative haze, they chatted with some men wearing three-cornered hats and green military coats. A man with small pox scars glared at them. They saw a servant shaking sheets from a window of a building. A woman in an old-fashioned dress sat in a chair sketching near an old plough. Anne and Eleanor were confused by the odd people wearing outdated clothes, but they figured people in Paris were just weird.

The ladies kept wandering until they got to the back of a building. A footman came through a door, spotted the women, and told them to hurry back to the main castle. The women had no idea why he would say such a thing, but they walked around to the front of what they would discover was the Petit Trianon. There was a wedding party there, and the ladies were relieved to feel the deep depression lifting. They toured the small castle and then left the grounds.

That wasn't the end of the story, though. Anne and Eleanor continued their vacation without discussing the weird afternoon in the Petit Trianon gardens. A few weeks later, they broached the subject. They discovered that they'd each experienced something unusual — that weird feeling — so they each wrote down what they saw. After comparing their notes, they discovered that they agreed on the basic details of what they had experienced except for one key point: Anne saw the sketcher but Eleanor said she simply *felt* the presence of the woman sketching. Nevertheless, they both believed that something strange had happened.

Further research on their part revealed that the ladies had visited the grounds on the anniversary of the 1792 massacre of Louis XVI and Marie Antoinette's Swiss Guard. Louis and Marie were locked in the Hall of the Assembly during this tragic event. Anne and Eleanor came to a startlingly conclusion: They had seen ghosts! That hypothesis seemed even more likely when they looked at a picture of Marie Antoinette and realized she was the woman sketching in the Petit Trianon gardens. On top of that, the ladies discovered that Marie had been sketching in the gardens in 1789 when she was told that the mob from Paris was on its way.

Eleanor was determined to learn more about this strange turn of events, so she went back to Versailles in January of the next year. She was floored to discover that the grounds were different from what she had remembered from her first visit. Back in England, the ladies tried to put the pieces together of what they saw. In 1911 they published a book called *An Adventure*, though they used the pen names Miss Morison and Miss Lamont. They were both high-bred daughters of clergymen, so they probably felt they had a certain reputation to uphold. It was only after their deaths that they were revealed as the writers of the very popular book. (Eleanor died in 1924 and Anne died in 1937.)

FOLIE À DEUX

Sometimes called shared psychotic disorder, folie à deux (literally, "the folly of two") is a condition in which a mentally healthy person believes the same psychotic delusions as the mentally ill person. The condition is most common when two people are really close to each other, but one is significantly more dominant than the other. If the dominant one believes pumpkins are dancing in the kitchen after dark, the passive partner will begin to think the same thing if he or she has a shared psychotic disorder.

The book details all the strange occurrences the ladies encountered on that August day in 1901. They then offer evidence to prove that what they saw could not be explained outside of the supernatural realm. Here are some of their key points.

1. They saw a plough, but no plough had been on the grounds in 1909. There was, however, a plough on the grounds in 1789.
2. The men in the green coats and tri-cornered hats matched pictures of the Swiss Guard, the men who were massacred in 1789.
3. The bridge the ladies crossed didn't exist in 1901, but it was there in 1789.
4. The man with the small pox scars matched a picture of the Comte de Vaudreuil, Marie Antoinette's nemesis.
5. The building from which the servant was shaking out sheets was not there in 1901 when the ladies visited the grounds.
6. The footman closed a door that had been bolted shut by 1901. But it would have been there in 1789. He hurried the ladies back to the main castle because he knew what was coming — the angry mob from Paris.
7. The deep feeling of depression both ladies felt would make sense if they were just on the brink of a terrible event in history.
8. Don't forget that Marie Antoinette was outside sketching just before the massacre in 1789. And the ladies saw a sketching woman in 1901.

The book sold 13,000 copies, proving that readers had an appetite for this kind of tale. Supposed supernatural experiences were very common at the time, so Anne and Eleanor's book fed into that excitement.

Skeptics questioned the story — because it does seem pretty far-fetched — so the ladies released their 1901 notes to prove that they described what they saw without knowing additional information about that day. (Remember, though, that Eleanor was a history major, and both women were academics. Do you suppose they really didn't know anything about the history of the place they were visiting? That seems questionable.)

Eleanor and Anne spent every free moment of their lives after 1901 researching what they believed they saw. (In fact, they were so devoted to each other, they lived out the rest of their lives living and working together. They were even nicknamed "man & wife" by the servants.) They concluded that they hadn't time traveled, nor had they seen ghosts as the originally believed. They posited that they had actually entered Marie Antoinette's 1789 memory. (Of course that doesn't explain why they saw Marie if they were in her memory, but the ladies didn't address that plot hole, except that Eleanor didn't see the sketcher. Perhaps it was she who is in Marie's memory, and Anne was along for the ride. Who knows.)

As crazy as it sounds that two women could enter into the memory of Marie Antoinette, they seemed to have a pretty airtight story. How could they know so much about the castle and its grounds otherwise?

Enter a writer and critic named W.H. Salter. In 1950 (thirteen years after Anne's death), W.H. discovered Anne and Eleanor's notes. But guess what? They weren't written in 1901. They were written in 1906, a fact W.H. discovered by carefully examining Anne and Eleanor's scribbles and their correspondence with the Society of Psychical Research. They wrote about things that happened much later than 1901, which means one or both of them then post-dated the letters. Anne and Eleanor had five years to add all kinds of details to their story. What appeared to be an amazingly accurate knowledge of things they could not have known turned out to be an amazingly accurate description of things they'd researched in the French national archives!

It's possible that Anne and Eleanor didn't believe they were lying, though. It's entirely possible that one of them thought she saw something, and in her zeal to prove it, she embellished a story that they both began to believe. Later research on the ladies suggests that Eleanor suffered from paranoid delusions that she may have convinced Anne were real. Throughout her life, Eleanor experienced paranoia, believing that all sorts of strange things were happening to her. At one point, she believed a German spy was watching her every move at Oxford.

VERSAILLES IN FLORIDA?

A super-duper-rich couple in Florida is building a replica of Versailles. The couple, David and Jackie Siegel, recently resumed construction on their dream house. When it is finished, the "American Versailles" will include two movies theaters, thirty bathrooms, and a whopping nine kitchens. (Who can use more than one?) Jackie's closet alone is 4,000 square feet.

Quick: Go ask your parents how many square feet your house is. I bet it's not as big as Jackie's closet. She even has an elevator in there! I'll let you guess what the elevator is made out of. If you said, "I don't know what elevators are made out of, do you?" then I'd be forced to say nope, not a clue. So I'll save us some time and just tell you that Jackie's elevator is made out of gold. Who knew that was a thing?

As you've probably guessed already, many people speculated that Anne and Eleanor were lesbians. Critics at the time questioned their morality because, in those days, people who were gay were considered morally suspect. Regardless of the nature of their relationship, the women unquestionably loved each other — and loved each other deeply. It seems likely that Eleanor's mental illness fueled a fantasy that Anne desperately wanted to believe because she loved her. If you think about it like that, it's kind of romantic.

As Terry Castle, a literary critic, notes: Anne and Eleanor's story really wasn't a supernatural ghost story; it was a love story. •

THE LIAR:
STEPHEN VOLK

DATE: 1992
THE LIE: That he was investigating a haunted house
REASON: Because he wanted to entertain viewers

In early 1993 two boys were diagnosed by medical professionals with post-traumatic stress disorder (PTSD). The cause? They'd both watched a British Broadcasting Corporation (BBC) show called **Ghostwatch**. The show was a scripted supernatural drama shot in a documentary style, and it hewed so closely to a documentary that many viewers were convinced that it was real. Doctors believed these two young boys were traumatized by the show.

Ghostwatch remains one of the highest-rated TV specials in BBC history. It began as a six-part story written by **Stephen Volk**. He'd been asked by his agent to write a scary supernatural miniseries. He was game for it. He was a fan of supernatural stories himself, especially Bram Stoker's *Dracula* and the short stories of Edgar Allan Poe. He particularly liked stories that were presented as real, even though they had a supernatural basis.

The network was reluctant to commit to a whole miniseries, so they decided to cut Stephen's six-part story down to just the last episode. That episode was where a film crew goes to investigate a haunted house and encounters a malevolent ghost terrorizing a family. Stephen wanted it to feel real, but he never envisioned it as a hoax. He simply wanted the audience to feel "complicit" in the story, and he wanted to make a comment about the medium of TV, about the way it makes us feel like we're seeing reality even when we aren't.

The ninety-minute special aired on October 31, 1992, at 9:25 p.m. The show featured real journalists Craig Charles and Sarah Greene reporting from the house. Periodically, the show would cut back to the studio where viewers would see host Michael Parkinson, a person viewers recognized as a real TV personality. Another journalist, Mike Smith, was taking viewer calls on a hotline. Those calls were scripted. Also appearing in the show was Dr. Lin Pascoe, an expert parapsychologist. Dr. Lin was played by an actress. The show also included a skeptic from New York, Emilio Sylvestri, played by an actor, commenting via satellite. The "live" investigation of the house had actually been filmed months before, but the show led viewers to believe that the events were all happening in real time.

The house was on Foxhill Drive in North London. The address was fake, but the producers did film in a real house. The show told viewers that the house was occupied by a single mother named Pam Early and her daughters, Suzanne and Kim. Pam told the crew that they had been noticing weird things since they moved into the house in December of 1991. They had seen furniture moving and heard loud banging noises that sounded metallic. That banging led them to name their "ghost" Pipes.

Craig's interviews with the fake neighbors revealed that house had been haunted for a long time. A previous occupant had hanged himself because he believed he was possessed. He had twelve hungry cats that were gnawing on his body before he was found. (Gross, right?) Neighbors said that dogs and kids have disappeared all over the neighborhood. One neighbor even tried to perform an exorcism on the house, but he couldn't get rid of Pipes.

Sarah Greene, the real journalist who played the investigator in the house, was just about to leave the house, believing that it was not haunted, when a wet spot showed up on the carpet. Suddenly, loud cat sounds came from the walls, and Suzanne, one of the daughters, had unexplained scratches all over her body. The banging and the cat noises kept getting louder, and there appeared to be a ghost upstairs. Before they could get out of the house, a picture fell off the wall, and Suzanne began speaking in a voice not her own. She was being possessed by Pipes. Everyone left except Sarah, who stayed to help get Suzanne out.

The camera went dark then. Viewers were taken back to the studio. The host, Michael Parkinson, started talking in a weird voice. He too had been possessed by Pipes! Dr. Lin figured out what happened. By bringing all the TV viewers to the house, they had accidentally started a séance. They'd channeled and unleashed dark spirits on all of England.

On that scary note, the credits rolled. Viewers could easily see for themselves that the show was written by Stephen and included actors playing the mom and the daughters and other characters. But many viewers either ignored the credits or didn't see them. A lot of people freaked out.

How many people freaked out is still a contested number. We know that the show drew more than eleven million viewers. In fact, it was the eighth-rated show that week. Some reports say that anywhere between 100,000 to 500,000 people called in to praise the show, complain about it, or ask if it was true. Other reports say it was more like 800 calls, and that most people were calling to say they didn't like it.

Whatever the numbers, the show did get people talking. And it wasn't just the kids who were scared by the show and later diagnosed with PTSD. One woman wanted the show to replace her husband's pants. He apparently soiled himself while watching the program. (That's a man who has been heartily scared.)

Another viewer, eighteen-year-old Martin Denham, committed suicide on November 5. Martin was convinced that he was possessed. He had been absolutely obsessed with the show after seeing it. Martin's mother and stepfather, April and Percy, blamed the show for his eventual suicide, but the coroner believed it was simply an unfortunate case of mental illness.

Though Stephen, the writer, never meant to fool viewers, he did manage to convince a lot of people that what they were seeing had some basis in reality. One of Stephen's close friends — who knew he wrote the program — believed it was true because she saw real newscasters. Funnily enough, Stephen hired real newscasters in the first place to make the show seem as real as possible.

You might think viewers in 1992 were kind of dumb, but you have to remember that it was a very different television landscape at that time. Reality TV wasn't everywhere the way it is now. Plus, the year 1992 was right after the first Gulf War. CNN had been relentlessly running war reports that felt like news and scripted drama mashed together. Now we are used to news reports that look like action movies, but that was all new in 1992.

The show was never shown again in the U.K., though clips have been released (you can find many of those on YouTube). The show has been rebroadcast in Canada and Belgium. And, of course, fans of the show or curious readers like you can buy it on DVD. In fact, super-fans participate

THE REST OF THE STORY

If you want to know more about Britain's "Halloween Hoax," check out a documentary on *Ghostwatch*. It's called *Ghostwatch: Behind the Curtains*. One caveat: It's only available in the U.K.

SEVEN "FACTS" ABOUT GHOSTS

It's hard to state any firm facts about ghosts because we don't even know if they exist. But hard-core ghost believers maintain that they know a few things about ghosts that are definitely true. Here's what they say.

1. Ghosts like pranks. (So ghosts are like annoying little brothers?)
2. Ghosts like to climb stairs at night.
3. Ghosts are cranky. (Well, yeah. They're dead. Wouldn't you be cranky?)
4. Ghosts can read your thoughts.
5. Ghosts can have a scent. (That's handy if you need to blame a certain smell on someone else. You know what I mean.)
6. Ghosts keep up with fashions of the day.
7. Ghosts can be animals too.

in something called National Séance. Every year at 9:25 p.m. on October 31, everyone plays his or her own *Ghostwatch* copy on TV.

So next Halloween if you hear wailing cats and Pipes clanking around your house, it might be because the National Séance awoke the spirits from the dead.

More likely, you are imagining things. •

CONCLUSION

So there you have it. More than forty people who told some really big, whopping lies. Yes, some lied for good reasons. That's true. But most told lies because they wanted money or power, or both.

Reading this book might make you a better liar, but I hope that's not what you take away from it. What's more important is that you recognize how to spot a liar so that you don't become a victim of one of these unscrupulous people.

Here's what you need to know to prepare for the liars you'll face in your lifetime.

1. It's easier for a liar to lie to you if you don't ask questions. Demand the evidence.
2. If something seems unlikely, it probably is.
3. Unexplained events are often very explainable. Look deeper. The evidence is often right in front of you.
4. Confidence doesn't mean that someone is honest. In fact, excessive confidence is often a tell that someone is lying.
5. Easy money doesn't exist. If it's too easy, you're probably getting fleeced. Trust me, there's no such thing as a magic money-making machine.
6. Absence of an immediate answer does not prove a supernatural explanation. It simply means you don't have an answer just yet.
7. Unfamiliar technology can be confusing at first. Don't confuse new technology with magic. Just because we don't understand it doesn't mean it has magical powers.
8. Satire is everywhere. Make sure you can recognize it. That's going to be important to understanding some of the greatest writing in all of history.
9. Lying is sometimes useful, as long as it doesn't hurt anyone.
10. The biggest lies you tell are to yourself. If you can't give up lying cold turkey, at least stop lying to yourself.

Trust me on all these things.
I wouldn't lie to you.

— CHRISTINE SEIFERT

FURTHER READING

If you want to learn more about liars, scam artists, pretenders, and hoax-sters, you are in luck. You'll find lots of great books in your library burst-ing with stories you have to read to believe. The books listed here are my favorite biographies, autobiographies, and narratives about liars, fakers, and scammers, some of whom are a lot like you and me. Others have lived amazing lives, the sort of lives we can only imagine.

Other books in this list tell us why we humans are so eager to believe liars, even when we should know better. (Hint: Part of our problem is that we are just lazy.) The writers of these books will help you develop the tools you need to make sure you have a well-exercised mind ready to spot a liar from a mile away. You'll be a regular human lie-detector.

Biographies, Autobiographies, and Narratives

Barnum, P.T. *The Life of P.T. Barnum*. Internet Archive. 1888. Accessed February 10, 2015. https://archive.org/details/lifeofptbarnum00barn.

You'd be hard-pressed to find a person who had more energy and more imagination than P.T. Barnum. It seems his entire life was spent dreaming up ways to make money, usually by tricking people who weren't very bright. His autobiography is an entertaining ride through his life, a life he was very proud of leading. When you finish reading it, you'll know why he's still considered one of the greatest showmen who ever lived.

Berkin, Carol. *Revolutionary Mothers: Women in the Struggle for America's Independence*. New York: Knopf, 2005.

If you think the Revolutionary War was won by men, you are wrong. Alongside all those soldiers were mothers, wives, daughters, and sisters fighting, organizing, and rallying. Not all of them had to lie about their identities, but few of them are remembered now for their contributions to the birth of America. Read this book to learn more about the women we've forgotten. Many might have lied in order to pass as men, but they did it for a greater cause. These women prove that sometimes lying is the best policy.

Clancy, Susan A. *Abducted: How People Come to Believe They Were Kidnapped by Aliens*. Cambridge, MA: Harvard University Press, 2005.

Believing you were abducted by aliens doesn't necessarily mean you are crazy. The world is full of perfectly sane people who legitimately believe they've been probed by aliens, in spite of massive evidence that such a thing has never, ever happened. So why does the alien abduction fantasy persist? Read this book and find out. (Hint: Our memories are funny little things, and it doesn't take much to twist them all up until they produce little green alien creatures.)

Gorenfeld, John. *Bad Moon Rising: How the Reverend Sun Myung Moon Created the Washington Times, Seduced the Religious Right, and Built His Kingdom*. Sausalito, CA: PoliPointPress, 2008.

If you want to read about someone who had more money than you can even imagine, check out this book about Sun Myung Moon. This guy knew how to play people, and he built an empire on the backs of trusting believers. To this day, Sun Myung's followers, the Moonies, control everything from a major newspaper to a multi-million dollar fishing industry.

Johnson, James Francis, and Floyd Miller. *The Man Who Sold the Eiffel Tower*. Garden City, NY: Doubleday, 1961.

You've probably heard a wily salesperson described as someone could sell sand in a desert, or snow shovels in hell, or ice to an Inuit. Well, Victor Lustig was one of those salesmen. He was so good, he warranted a whole book about his scams. If you think you're good at persuasion, just wait until you see the strategies Victor developed and used on unsuspecting victims all the way around the world.

Massie, Robert K. *The Romanovs: The Final Chapter*. New York: Random House, 1995.

The story of the Romanovs is fascinating and tragic. They were young, beautiful, enviable royalty who lived lives we can only imagine. But they were brutally murdered by soldiers carrying out an uprising against the royal family. Young Anastasia's missing body gave people hope that she had escaped and was out there somewhere. Anna Anderson ignited that hope by convincing people that maybe little Anastasia, beloved princess, had defied the odds and survived. DNA tests, almost a hundred years later, finally revealed the truth: Anna Anderson was a fraud, a liar in princess's clothes.

Saint-Andre, Nathaniel, and John Clarke. *A Short Narrative of an Extraordinary Delivery of Rabbets Perform'd by Mr. John Howard Surgeon at Guilford. Published by Mr. St. Andre Surgeon and Anatomist to His Majesty*. The 2nd ed. London: Printed for John Clarke, at the Bible under the Royal-Exchange, 1727.

If you wonder how someone like Mary Toft could fool doctors about giving birth to rabbits, then I suggest you read this book. Mary was a creative woman who took advantage of the fact that men, even men who were doctors, didn't always know that much about the female body. Read all about how she pulled off this disgusting stunt.

Stewart, Doug. *The Boy Who Would Be Shakespeare: A Tale of Forgery and Folly*. Cambridge, MA: Da Capo Press, 2010.

Who knew a story of forgery could be so much fun? Well, Doug Stewart did. In this book, he tells the complete story of William Henry Ireland, the young son who simply wanted his father's love. That desire led to one of the biggest forgery scandals in all of history. Learn how William pulled off the stunt as long as he did. (Hint: It involved a father who was so desperate to believe he'd gotten his hands on a real Shakespeare manuscript that he let reason fly out the window.)

Zuckoff, Mitchell. *Ponzi's Scheme: The True Story of a Financial Legend*. New York: Random House, 2005.

> *Charles Ponzi might have been a crook, but he was a brilliant man who knew exactly how to make people like him. In fact, he made people like him so much that they basically handed over their money — no questions asked. And that's the primary necessity for a Ponzi Scheme: People have to be willing to give you money in the belief that you will give them back even more. Mitchell's lively book about Charles is the story behind the legendary man whose name would eventually become synonymous with financial fraud.*

Books That Will Sharpen Your Lie-detecting Skills

Marchand, Roland. *Advertising the American Dream: Making Way for Modernity, 1920–1940*. Berkeley: University of California Press, 1985.

> *Advertising may be the ultimate lie. It convinces us that we need useless products to make us happy, and yet once we acquire those things, advertising tells us we need more. Even if you think you are immune to advertising, you aren't. Billions of dollars make up the advertising industry, which means thousands and thousands of smart people are constantly coming up with new ways to make you think you need just the right useless stuff to achieve the American Dream.*

Randi, James. *The Faith Healers*. Buffalo, NY: Prometheus Books, 1989.

> *Faith healers are people who claim to have God-given powers to heal the sick and inform. I say "claim" because James Randi's book introduces you to a whole lot of faith healers who are proven frauds. Even so, they continue to prey on people who are often at the lowest point of their lives. James gives a solid "shame on you" to the frauds who take money from those less fortunate as a means to further their own careers and build empires under the guise of religion.*

Sagan, Carl, and Ann Druyan. *The Demon-Haunted World: Science as a Candle in the Dark*. New York: Random House, 1996.

> *Carl Sagan may be the most famous and important astronomer to ever live, outside of Galileo. Carl wrote a lot of books about science, but this one is about pseudoscience. Pseudoscience is basically fake science. It might look like science or use the same language as science, but it's illogical, unsubstantiated, and often dangerous. Carl and his wife, Ann, provide strategies for combatting pseudoscience.*

Shermer, Michael. *Why People Believe Weird Things: Pseudoscience, Superstition, and Other Confusions of Our Time*. New York: W.H. Freeman, 1997.

> *Michael Shermer is a writer who wondered why people continue to believe unbelievable things, even after they are presented with loads of credible evidence to the contrary. It turns out that we human beings are not always rational creatures. The fact that we don't always rely on the logical part of our brain is why it's so easy for tricksters and scam artists to fool us. Michael provides fascinating information about how we are fooled and what we can do to be better prepared against liars.*

Books are great, but you'll also find additional materials with just a couple of keystrokes. The sites listed here are excellent resources for learning even more about history's biggest liars and lies. All are maintained and updated based on reputable sources; in fact, you'll probably find a lot of other materials you'll want to read after browsing these sites. You'll be an expert on lies and liars in no time.

Web Sites

Bio.com. Accessed February 10, 2015. http://www.biography.com/.

The brief biographies of your favorite liars are just keystrokes away. Check out this site for historical information on any famous liar you can think of.

The Museum of Hoaxes. Accessed February 10, 2015. http://www.hoaxes.org/.

Hoaxes are as old as human history itself. If you want to learn about every hoax under the sun, check out this site.

The Museum of UnNatural Mystery. Accessed February 10, 2015.
 http://www.unmuseum.org.

Some of the biggest hoaxes ever pulled have to do with aliens and UFOs. If you want to learn about those hoaxes, visit this site. I bet you didn't realize how many people have lied about aliens and mysterious beings.

The Skeptic's Dictionary. Accessed February 10, 2015. http://www.skepdic.com/.

If you want to know more about pseudoscience, supernatural hoaxes, and paranormal fantasies, this is the site for you. The contributors will tell you about anything you could ever want to know from alien attacks to yetis and zombies.

REFERENCES

Section 1: Tall-Tale Tellers

Chapter 1: Hard-to-Believe-Anyone-Believed Stories

Mary Toft

The Curious Case of Mary Toft. London, 1726. Sp Coll Hunterian Aa.7.20 and other works. University Glasgow Library Special Collections Department, Aug. 2009. Web. 17 Mar. 2014. <http://special.lib. gla.ac.uk/exhibns/month/aug2009.html>.

Howell, Michael, and Peter Ford. *The True History of the Elephant Man*. London: Allison & Busby, 2007.

Leafe, David. "The child savage kept as a pet by King George." *Daily Mail*. Associated Newspapers, 23 Mar. 2011. Web. 17 Mar. 2014. <http://www.dailymail. co.uk/news/article-1369387/The-child-savage-kept-pet-King-George.html>.

Russell, Niki. "Mary Toft and Her Extraordinary Delivery of Rabbits." *The Public Domain Review*. N.p., n.d. Web. 17 Mar. 2014. <http://publicdomainreview. org/2013/03/20/mary-toft-and-her-extraordinary-delivery-of-rabbits/>.

Saint-Andre, Nathaniel, and John Clarke. *A Short Narrative of an Extraordinary Delivery of Rabbets: Perform'd by Mr John Howard, Surgeon at Guilford*. London, Printed for John Clarke, at the Bible under the Royal-Exchange. MDCCXXVII: n.p., 1727. Boston Public Library. Web. 17 Mar. 2014. <https://archive.org/ details/shortnarrativeof00sain>.

Todd, Dennis. *Imagining Monsters: Miscreations of the Self in Eighteenth-Century England*. Chicago: University of Chicago, 1995.

Jonathan Swift

Conolly, Leonard, et al., eds. "Jonathan Swift." *The Broadview Anthology of British Literature: The Restoration and the Eighteenth Century*. Vol. 3. Peterborough, Ont.: Broadview, 2006. 302–04.

Landa, Louis A. "'A Modest Proposal' and Populousness." *Modern Philology*. 40.2. (1942): 161. JSTOR. Web. 17 Mar. 2014.

Phiddian, Robert. "Have You Eaten Yet? The Reader in 'A Modest Proposal.'" *Studies in English Literature 1500–1900*. Vol. 36, No. 3, Restoration and Eighteenth Century (1996): 603-21. JSTOR. Web. 17 Mar. 2014.

Swift, Jonathan. *The Benefit of Farting Explained, Or, The Fundament-all Cause of the Distempers Incident to the Fair Sex*. Exeter: Old Abbey, 1996. Print.

Swift, Jonathan. "A Modest Proposal." The Project Gutenberg, 27 Jul. 2008. Web. 17 Mar. 2014. <http://www.gutenberg.org/files/1080/1080-h/1080-h.htm>.

P.T. Barnum

Barnum, P.T. *The Life of P.T. Barnum Written by Himself, Including his Golden Rules for Money-Making*. Buffalo: Courier Co., 1888. Web. 28 Oct. 2014. <https:// archive.org/details/lifeofptbarnum00barn>.

"The Feejee Mermaid, 1842." *The Museum of Hoaxes*. Alex Boese, 2002.Web. 28 Oct. 2014. <http://hoaxes. org/archive/permalink/the_feejee_mermaid>.

"The Hoaxes of P.T. Barnum." *The Museum of Hoaxes*. Alex Boese, 2002. Web. 28 Oct. 2014. <http://hoaxes. org/archive/display/category/p.t._barnum>.

Maher, Kathleen. "P.T. Barnum, (1810-1891) – The Man, the Myth, the Legend." *The Barnum Museum*. Web. 28 Oct. 2014. <http://www.barnum-museum. org/manmythlegend.htm>.

"Pondering Pachyderms." *Center for Elephant Conservation*. Web. 9 Feb. 2015. <http://www.elephantcenter. com/asian-elephant-facts/pondering-pachyderms/>.

"P.T. Barnum." *Bio*. A&E Television Networks, 2015. Web. 28 Oct. 2014. <http://www.biography.com/ people/pt-barnum-9199751#death-and-legacy>.

"PT Barnum, The Shakespeare of Advertising." *PT Barnum*. Web. 28 Oct. 2014. <http://www.ptbarnum. org/humbugs.html>.

Chapter 2: Exotic Fabrications

George Psalmanazar

"George Psalmanazar the Celebrated Native of Formosa." *Forging a Collection*, University of Delaware Library Special Collections Department. Web. 28 Oct. 2014. <http://www.lib.udel.edu/ud/spec/exhibits/forgery/psalm.htm>.

Lynch, Jack. "Orientalism as Performance Art: The Strange Case of George Psalmanazar." *Rutgers University*. Lecture at CUNY Seminar on Eighteenth-Century Literature, delivered 29 Jan. 1999. Web. 28 Oct. 2014. <http://andromeda.rutgers.edu/~jlynch/ Papers/psalm.html>.

"The Native of Formosa." *The Museum of Hoaxes*. Alex Boese, 2002. Web. 28 Oct. 2014. <http://hoaxes.org/ formosa.html>.

Washington Irving

"Christopher Columbus Suffered From a Fatal Form of Arthritis." *University of Maryland Medical Center*. 6 May 2005. UMMC, 2015. Web. 9 Feb. 2015. <http://umm.edu/news-and-events/news-releases/2005/christopher-columbus-suffered-from-a-fatal-form-of-arthritis>.

"Columbus in History." *University of Virginia*. Web. 9 Feb. 2015. <http://xroads.virginia.edu/~cap/columbus/col3.html>.

Hazlett, John D. "Literary Nationalism and Ambivalence in Washington Irving's The Life and Voyages of Christopher Columbus." *American Literature: A Journal of Literary History, Criticism, and Bibliography.* 55.4 (1983): 560–75. <http://scholarworks.uno.edu/cgi/viewcontent.cgi?article=1002&context=engl_facpubs>.

Irving, Washington. *A History of the Life and Voyages of Christopher Columbus.* G. & C. Carvill, 1828. <https://archive.org/details/ahistorylifeand08irvigoog>.

Russell, Jeffrey Burton. *Inventing the Flat Earth: Columbus and Modern Historians.* Westport, CT: Praeger, 1997.

Shreve, Jack. "Christopher Columbus: A Bibliographic Voyage." *Choice.* Vol. 29. Jan. 1991. 703–11. <http://libertyparkusafd.org/lp/Columbus/papers%5CChristopher%20Columbus%20-%20%20A%20Bibliographic%20Voyage.htm>.

Strauss, Valerie. "Christopher Columbus: 3 things you think he did that he didn't." *The Washington Post.* 14 Oct. 2013. The Washington Post, 2015. Web. 25 Feb. 2015. <http://www.washingtonpost.com/blogs/answer-sheet/wp/2013/10/14/christopher-columbus-3-things-you-think-he-did-that-he-didnt/>.

"Washington Irving." *Bio.* A&E Television Networks, 2015. Web. 9 Feb. 2015. <http://www.biography.com/people/washington-irving-9350087#profile>.

King Tut

"The Curse of the Mummy." *KingTutOne.Com.* Web. 9 Feb. 2015. <http://www.kingtutone.com/tutankhamun/curse/>.

Krystek, Lee. "Howard Carter and the Curse of Tut's Mummy." *The Museum of UnNatural Mystery.* Web. 9 Feb. 2015. <http://www.unmuseum.org/mummy.htm>.

"Mummies Facts." 2015. *The History Channel website.* 9 Feb. 2015. <http://www.history.com/interactives/mummies-facts-infographic>.

Peters, Scott. "Amazing MUMMY Facts (The ULTIMATE Mummy Fact Guide!)" *Egypt About.* 2013. Web. 9 Feb. 2015. <http://www.egyptabout.com/2013/07/101-mummy-facts-ultimate-mummy-fact.html>.

Peters, Scott. "5 Ancient Mummy Jokes." *Egypt About.* 2013. Web. 9 Feb. 2015. <http://www.egyptabout.com/2013/05/5-ancient-egypt-mummy-jokes.html>.

Smithsonian Journeys. "The Curse of King Tut's Tomb." *Smithsonian Journeys.* 17 Aug. 2010. Smithsonian Journeys, 2015. Web. 25 Feb. 2015. <http://www.smithsonianjourneys.org/blog/the-curse-of-king-tuts-tomb-180950898/>.

Chapter 3: Horseplay

Trojan Horse

"Did the Trojan War Really Happen?" *University of Cincinnati.* Troia Projekt and CERHAS. Web. 9 Feb. 2015. <http://cerhas.uc.edu/troy/q404.html>.

Gill, N.S. "Helen of Troy." *About Education.* About.com, 2015. Web. 9 Feb. 2015. <http://ancienthistory.about.com/cs/troyilium/a/helenoftroybasc.htm>.

Gill, N.S. "The Trojan War and the Trojan Horse." *About Education.* About.com, 2015. Web. 9 Feb. 2015. <http://ancienthistory.about.com/cs/troyilium/a/taleoftroy_3.htm>.

"Homer." *Poets.org.* Academy of American Poets. Web. 9 Feb. 2015. <http://www.poets.org/poetsorg/poet/homer>.

"Homer." *The Literature Network.* Jalic Inc., 2015. Web. 9 Feb. 2015. <http://www.online-literature.com/homer/>.

"Trojan Horse." *Encyclopædia Britannica. Encyclopædia Britannica Online.* Encyclopædia Britannica Inc., 2015. Web. 9 Feb. 2015. <http://www.britannica.com/EBchecked/topic/606297/Trojan-horse>.

"Trojan Horse or Trojan: It's Not All a Myth." *Antivirus.com.* 2013. Web. 9 Feb. 2015. <http://www.antivirus.com/security-software/definition/trojan-horse/>.

"The Trojan War." *Mortal Women of the Trojan War.* Stanford University. Web. 9 Feb. 2015. <http://web.stanford.edu/~plomio/history.html#anchor204279>.

Clever Hans

"Clever Hans Phenomenon." *The Skeptic's Dictionary.* 2015. Web. 9 Feb. 2015. <http://skepdic.com/cleverhans.html>.

Grimm, Jacob, and Wilhelm Grimm. "Clever Hans." *Children's and Household Tales – Grimms' Fairy Tales.* No. 32. 1812. Translated by D.L. Ashliman. 2002. <http://www.pitt.edu/~dash/grimm032.html>.

Jones, Tegan. "The Horse That Could Do Math: The Unintentional Clever Hans Hoax." *Today I Found Out.* Vacca Foeda Media, 2012. Web. 9 Feb. 2015. <http://www.todayifoundout.com/index.php/2013/12/horse-math-unintentional-clever-hans-hoax/>.

"The Story of Clever Hans." *KBR Horse Training Information.* 1997. Web. 9 Feb. 2015. <http://www.kbrhorse.net/tra/hans.html>.

Chapter 4: Stinkin' Stories

Millard Fillmore

Adams, Cecil. "Where Can I Join the Millard Fillmore Society?" *The Straight Dope.* 13 Feb. 1976. Sun-Times Media, 2015. Web. 25 Feb. 2015. <http://www.straightdope.com/columns/read/98/where-can-i-join-the-millard-fillmore-society>.

"Mencken's History of the Bathtub." *The Museum of Hoaxes*. Alex Boese, 2014. Web. 9 Feb. 2015. <http://hoaxes.org/archive/permalink/the_history_of_the_bathtub>.

"Millard Fillmore's Bathtub." *Sniggle.net*. Web. 9 Feb. 2015. <https://sniggle.net/bathtub.php>.

"A neglected 91st anniversary of Mencken and Millard Fillmore's Bathtub." *Timpanogos.wordpress.com*. Web. 9 Feb. 2015. <https://timpanogos.wordpress.com/2008/12/28/a-neglected-91st-anniversary-of-mencken-and-millard-fillmores-bathtub/>.

"President Zachary Taylor dies unexpectedly." 2015. *The History Channel website*. 9 Feb. 2015. <http://www.history.com/this-day-in-history/president-zachary-taylor-dies-unexpectedly>.

"United States Presidential Election of 1848. United States Government." *Encyclopædia Britannica. Encyclopædia Britannica Online*. Encyclopædia Britannica Inc., 2015.Web. 25 Feb. 2015.http://www.britannica.com/EBchecked/topic/1770963/United-States-presidential-election-of-1848.

Listerine

719woman.com. "Alternative Uses of Mouthwash." *MomsEveryday*. Gray Television, 2015. Web. 9 Feb. 2015. <http://www.momseveryday.com/home/momtomom/719woman/headlines/Alternative-Uses-for-Mouthwash-241978081.html>.

Fine, Daniel H. "Listerine: past, present and future — a test of thyme." *Journal of Dentistry*. June 2010. Elsevier, 2010. <http://www.jodjournal.com/article/S0300-5712(10)70003-8/abstract>.

Levitt, Steven D., and Stephen J. Dubner. *Freakonomics: A Rogue Economist Explores the Hidden Side of Everything*. New York. Harper Perennial, 2009.

"Listerine." *Cracked.com*. Demand Media, 2013. Web. 9 Feb. 2015. <http://www.cracked.com/funny-8228-listerine/>.

"Listerine Gests Rid of Dandruff." *Popular Science Monthly*. May 1930. 116(5): 17 (ad).

Marchand, Roland. *Advertising the American Dream: Making Way for Modernity, 1920–1940*. Berkeley: University of California Press , 1985.

O'Malley, Michael. "Understanding Advertising." *Exploring US History*. Apr. 2004. Web. 9 Feb. 2015. <http://chnm.gmu.edu/exploring/20thcentury/understandingadvertising/>.

"The Too-Good-to-Be-True Product Hall of Fame." *Time.com*. 6 Oct. 2011. Time Inc., 2015. <http://business.time.com/2011/10/11/14-products-with-notoriously-misleading-advertising-claims/slide/listerine/>.

Japanese Poop Burgers

Arumugam, Nadia. "Meat Made from Human Feces: Hoax or Japan's Best New Invention?" *Forbes*. 8 Jul. 2011. Forbes.com, 2015. Web. 25 Feb. 2015. <http://www.forbes.com/sites/nadiaarumugam/2011/07/08/meat-made-from-human-feces-hoax-or-japans-best-new-invention/>.

Elliott, Justin. "The mystery of the Japanese 'poop burger' story." *Salon*. 23 Jun. 2011. Salon Media Group, 2015. Web. 25 Feb. 2015. <http://www.salon.com/2011/06/23/japan_feces_meat_viral/>.

"Facts About Poop." *SmellyPoop.com*. Web. 9 Feb. 2015. <http://www.smellypoop.com/facts_about_poop.php>.

Matyszczyk, Chris. "Japanese scientist creates 'poop burger'? Surely Not." *Cnet.com*. 18 Jun. 2011. CBS Interactive, 2015. Web. 25 Feb. 2015. <http://www.cnet.com/news/japanese-scientist-creates-poop-burger-surely-not/>.

News Corp Australian Papers. "Japanese Scientists Create Meat From Poop." *FoxNews*. 17 Jun. 2011. FOX News Network, 2015. Web. 25 Feb. 2015. <http://www.foxnews.com/scitech/2011/06/17/japanese-scientists-create-meat-from-poop/>.

Section 2: Great Pretenders

Chapter 5: Fakers

Mattie Griffith

Andrews, William L. "Martha Griffith Browne, d. 1906." *Documenting the American South*. University Library, The University of North Carolina at Chapel Hill, 2004. Web. 9 Feb. 2015. <http://docsouth.unc.edu/neh/browne/bio.html>.

Douglass, Frederick. *The Narrative of the Life of Frederick Douglass An American Slave*. Project Gutenberg. 10 Jan. 2006. Web. 9 Feb. 2015. <http://www.gutenberg.org/files/23/23-h/23-h.htm>.

"Hidden Facts about Slavery in America." *The New Observer*. 17 Jun. 2013. The New Observer, 2015. Web. 25 Feb. 2015. <http://newobserveronline.com/hidden-facts-about-slavery-in-america/>.

Lockard, Joe. "Griffith Browne, Mattie." *American National Biography Online*. October 2007. American Council of Learned Societies. Oxford University Press, 2007. Web. 9 Feb. 2015. <http://www.anb.org/articles/16/16-03522.html>.

Lockard, Joe. "Passing Away, or Narrative Transvestism as Social Metaphor in Multiethnic Societies." *Re-Placing America: Conversations and Contestations: Selected Essays*. Ed. Ruth Hsu, Cynthia G. Franklin, and Suzanne Kosanke. Honolulu: University of Hawai'I, 2000. 204.

Mintz, Steven. "Facts About the Slave Trade and Slavery." *The Gilder Lehrman Institute of American History.* 2015. Web. 9 Feb. 2015. <http://www.gilderlehrman. org/history-by-era/slavery-and-anti-slavery/resources/ facts-about-slave-trade-and-slavery>.

"Slave narrative." *Encyclopædia Britannica. Encyclopædia Britannica Online.* Encyclopædia Britannica Inc., 2015. Web. 9 Feb. 2015. <http://www.britannica. com/EBchecked/topic/548224/slave-narrative>.

William Henry Ireland

"100 Facts About William Shakespeare." *Absolute Shakespeare.* Web. 9 Feb. 2015. <http://absoluteshakespeare. tripod.com/homepage/id1.html.>

Noble, Joseph Veach. "Forgery." *Encyclopædia Britannica. Encyclopædia Britannica Online.* Encyclopædia Britannica Inc., 2015. Web. 9 Feb. 2015. <http:// www.britannica.com/EBchecked/topic/213587/forgery/69716/Detection-of-forgeries-in-the-visual-arts>.

"Shakespeare's Life." *Folger Shakespeare Library.* Web. 9 Feb. 2015. <http://www.folger.edu/template. cfm?cid=1583>.

Stewart, Doug. *The Boy Who Would Be Shakespeare: A Tale of Forgery and Folly.* Cambridge, MA: Da Capo Press, 2010.

"William Henry Ireland and the Shakespeare Fabrication." *Forging a Collection.* University of Delaware Library Special Collections Department. Web. 9 Feb. 2015. <http://www.lib.udel.edu/ud/spec/exhibits/ forgery/ireland.htm>.

"William-Henry Ireland's Great Shakespearean Hoax." *NPR.* 19 Jun. 2010. NPR, 2015. Web. 25 Feb. 2015. <http://www.npr.org/templates/story/story. php?storyId=127931669>.

Frank Abagnale

Bell, Rachael. "Skywayman: The Story of Frank W. Abagnale Jr." *Crime Library.* Turner Entertainment Networks, 2015. Web. 9 Feb. 2015. <http://www. crimelibrary.com/criminal_mind/scams/frank_abagnale/index.html>.

"Frank Abagnale." *Bio.* A&E Television Networks, 2015. Web. 9 Feb. 2015. <http://www.biography. com/people/frank-abagnale-20657335>.

Hunt, Stephanie. "Charleston Profile: Bona Fide." *Charleston Mag.* Sep. 2010. Web. 9 Feb. 2015. <http://www.abagnale.com/news092010.asp>.

Solon, Olivia. "Frank Abagnale on the death of the con artist and the rise of cybercrime." *Wired.co.uk.* 4 Mar. 2013. Wired, 2015. Web. 25 Feb. 2015. <http:// www.wired.co.uk/news/archive/2013-03/04/frankabagnale>.

Milli Vanilli

Hess, Mike. "Milli Vanilli, the Real Story – 20 Years Later." *PopEater.* 29 Jan. 2010. AOL, 2015. Web. 25 Feb. 2015. <http://www.popeater.com/2010/01/29/ milli-vanilli-fab-morvan-grammy/>.

Huey, Steve. "Milli Vanilli." *AllMusic.* AllMusic, 2015. Web. 9 Feb. 2015. <http://www.allmusic.com/artist/ milli-vanilli-mn0000412710/biography>.

Kelly, Katie. "11 Times It Was Painfully Obvious That Famous Singers Were Lip-Syncing." *Pigeons and Planes.* 3 Jul. 2013. <http://pigeonsandplanes. com/2013/07/lip-syncing-famous-singers/>.

"Milli Vanilli Fan Club Facebook page." Web. 9 Feb. 2015. <https://www.facebook.com/pages/Milli-Vanilli-Fan-Club/195412967150845>.

Pizac, Douglas C. "Famous Lip-syncers." *Timesunion. com.* 23 Jan. 2013. The Hearst Corporation, 2015. Web. 25 Feb. 2015. <http://www.timesunion.com/ news/slideshow/Famous-Lip-syncers-55599.php>.

James Frey

Barton, Laura. "The man who rewrote his life." *The Guardian.* 15 Sep. 2006. Guardian News and Media, 2015. Web. 25 Feb. 2015. <http://www.theguardian. com/books/2006/sep/15/usa.world>.

Caesar, Julius. *The Gallic Wars.* Translated by W.A. McDevitte and W.S. Bohn. *The Internet Classics Archive.* Daniel C. Stevenson, Web Atomics, 2000. <http://classics.mit.edu/Caesar/gallic.mb.txt>.

Flood, Alison. "James Frey wins $2m deal for young adult SF novel." *The Guardian.* 15 Jan. 2014. Guardian News and Media, 2015. Web. 25 Feb. 2015. <http://www.theguardian.com/books/2014/jan/15/ james-frey-2m-deal-young-adult-sf-novel>.

Frey, James. *A Million Little Pieces.* New York: Anchor Books, 2005.

"A Million Little Lies." *The Smoking Gun.* 4 Jan. 2006. TSG, 2015. Web. 25 Feb. 2015. <http://www. thesmokinggun.com/documents/celebrity/million-little-lies>.

"Oprah's Book Club: The Complete List." *Oprah.* Harpo Productions, 2015. Web. 9 Feb. 2015. <http://www.oprah.com/book/The-Invention-of-Wings?editors_pick_id=26790>.

Peretz, Evgenia. "James Frey's Morning After." *Vanity Fair.* Jun. 2008. Conde Nast. Web. 25 Feb. 2015. <http://www.vanityfair.com/culture/features/2008/06/ frey200806>.

Mesh Flinders

Davis, Joshua. "The Secret World of Lonelygirl." *Wired.* Dec. 2006. Wired.com, 2009. Web. 25 Feb. 2015. <http://archive.wired.com/wired/archive/14.12/lonelygirl.html>.

Heffernan, Virginia, and Tom Zeller. "The Lonelygirl That Really Wasn't." *The New York Times.* 13 Sept. 2006. The New York Times Co., 2015. Web. 25 Feb. 2015. http://www.nytimes.com/2006/09/13/ technology/13lonely.html?_r=1&.

Flinders, Mesh. "Lonelygirl15 Channel." Online video. *YouTube.* 12 May 2006. Web. 25 Feb. 2015. <https:// www.youtube.com/user/lonelygirl15>.

"Lonelygirl15." *Know Your Meme.* Cheezburger, Inc., 2015. Web. 11 Feb. 2015. <http://knowyourmeme.com/memes/lonelygirl15>.

Phelan, Jessica. "25 biggest moments in Internet history." *Salon.* 14 Mar. 2014. Salon Media Group, 2015. Web. 25 Feb. 2015. <http://www.salon.com/2014/03/14/25_biggest_moments_in_internet_history_partner/>.

Wei, Will. "WHERE ARE THEY NOW? Creators Of 'Lonelygirl15' Turned Web Series Into A Multi-Million Dollar Company." *Business Insider.* 20, Jul. 2010. Business Insider Inc., 2015. Web. 25 Feb. 2015. <http://www.businessinsider.com/where-are-they-now-creators-of-lonelygirl15-turned-web-series-into-a-multi-million-dollar-company-2010-7>.

Chapter 6: Inheritance Seekers

Cassie Chadwick

Abbott, Karen. "The High Priestess of Fraudulent Finance." *Smithsonian.com.* 27 Jun. 2012. Smithsonian, 2015. Web. 25 Feb. 2015. <http://www.smithsonianmag.com/history/the-high-priestess-of-fraudulent-finance-45/?no-ist>.

"Andrew Carnegie: The Gospel of Wealth, 1889." *Internet Modern History Sourcebook.* Paul Halsall, Aug. 1997. Web. 11 Feb. 2015. <http://legacy.fordham.edu/halsall/mod/1889carnegie.asp>.

Crosbie, John S. *The Incredible Mrs. Chadwick: The most notorious woman of her age.* McGraw-Hill Ryerson, 1975.

Segrave, Kerry. *Women Swindlers in America 1860-1920.* New York: McGraw McFarland & Company, 2007.

Stamberg, Susan. "How Andrew Carnegie Turned His Fortune Into A Library Legacy." *NPR.* 1 Aug. 2013. NPR, 2015. Web. 25 Feb. 2015. <http://www.npr.org/2013/08/01/207272849/how-andrew-carnegie-turned-his-fortune-into-a-library-legacy>.

"Top 10 Imposters: Cassie Chadwick." *Time.* 26 May 2009. Time Inc., 2014. Web. 25 Feb. 2015. <http://content.time.com/time/specials/packages/article/0,28804,1900621_1900618_1900852,00.html>.

Women in History. "Cassie L. Chadwick biography." *Women in History Ohio.* 26 Jan. 2013. Web. 25 Feb. 2015. <http://www.womeninhistoryohio.com/cassie-l-chadwick.html>.

Anna Anderson

Badkar, Mamta. "17 Mind-Blowing Facts About Russia." *Business Insider.* 10 Mar. 2014. Business Insider Inc., 2015. Web. 25 Feb. 2015. <http://www.businessinsider.com/17-mind-blowing-facts-about-russia-2014-3>.

Kurth, Peter. *Anastasia: The Riddle of Anna Anderson.* New York: Back Bay Books, 1985.

Massie, Robert K. *The Romanovs: The Final Chapter.* New York: Random House, 1996.

McClenagan, Ryan. "10 bizarre facts about Russia you probably didn't know." *The Daily Caller.* 17 Feb. 2014. The Daily Caller, 2015. Web. 25 Feb. 2015. <http://dailycaller.com/2014/02/17/10-bizarre-facts-about-russia-you-did-not-know-slideshow/>.

Pompilio, Natalie. "Anna Anderson: The Great Imposter." *Legacy.com.* 12 Feb. 2014. Legacy.com, 2015. Web. 25 Feb. 2015. <http://www.legacy.com/news/legends-and-legacies/anna-anderson-the-great-imposter/2005>.

"Top 10 Imposters: Anna Anderson." *Time.* 26 May 2009. Time Inc., 2014. Web. 25 Feb. 2015. <http://content.time.com/time/specials/packages/article/0,28804,1900621_1900618_1900620,00.html>.

Chapter 7: Lady Pirates and Soldiers

Anne Bonny and Mary Read

Defoe, Daniel. *A General History of the Pyrates: from their first rise and settlement in the island of Providence, to the present time.* Project Gutenberg, 2012. Web. 25 Feb. 2015. <http://www.gutenberg.org/files/40580/40580-h/40580-h.htm>.

Minster, Christopher. "Biography of Anne Bonny." *About Education.* About.com, 2015. Web. 11 Feb. 2015. <http://latinamericanhistory.about.com/od/historyofthecaribbean/p/Biography-Of-Anne-Bonny.htm>.

Minster, Christopher. "Biography of Mary Read." *About Education.* About.com, 2015. Web. 11 Feb. 2015. <http://latinamericanhistory.about.com/od/Pirates/p/Biography-Of-Mary-Read.htm>.

Pallardy, Richard. "Anne Bonny." *Encyclopædia Britannica. Encyclopædia Britannica Online.* Encyclopædia Britannica Inc., 2015. Web. 9 Feb. 2015. <http://www.britannica.com/EBchecked/topic/1558418/Anne-Bonny>.

Potter, Chris. "Why is our baseball team called the Pittsburgh Pirates? What do Pirates have to do with Pittsburgh?" *Pittsburgh City Paper.* 14 Aug. 2003. Pittsburgh City Paper, 2015. Web. 25 Feb. 2015. <http://www.pghcitypaper.com/pittsburgh/why-is-our-baseball-team-called-the-pittsburgh-pirates-what-do-pirates-have-to-do-with-pittsburgh/Content?oid=1335541>.

Deborah Sampson

American Revolutionary War Facts. Web. 11 Feb. 2015. <http://www.american-revolutionary-war-facts.com/>.

Berkin, Carol. *Revolutionary Mothers: Women in the Struggle for America's Independence.* New York: Knopf, 2005. Bois, Danuta. "Deborah Sampson." 1998. *Distinguished Women of Past and Present,* 2015. Web. 11 Feb. 2015. <http://www.distinguishedwomen.com/bio.php?womanid=2000>.

Keiter, Jane. "Deborah Sampson (1760-1827)." *National Women's History Museum*. Web. 11 Feb. 2015. <https://www.nwhm.org/education-resources/biography/biographies/deborah-sampson/>.

Leonard, Patrick J. "Deborah Samson." *Canton Massachusetts Historical Society*. 2006. Web. 11 Feb. 2015. <http://www.canton.org/samson/>.

"Revolutionary War." *Fact Monster*. Pearson Education, 2007. Web. 25 Feb. 2015. <http://www.factmonster.com/ipka/A0769969.html>.

"Ten Facts about Washington and the Revolutionary War." *George Washington's Mount Vernon*. Mount Vernon Ladies' Association, 2015. Web. 11 Feb. 2015. <http://www.mountvernon.org/george-washington/the-revolutionary-war/ten-facts-about-the-revolutionary-war/>.

"These 9 Facts About The American Revolution Will Prove You Know Nothing About It." *ViralNova*. 30 Aug. 2014. ViralNova, 2015. Web. 25 Feb. 2015. <http://www.viralnova.com/american-revolution/>.

Chapter 8: Pen-Named Writers

Ben Franklin

"Ben Franklin." *UShistory.org*. Independence Hall Association, 2014. Web. 11 Feb. 2015. <http://www.ushistory.org/franklin/>.

"Benjamin Franklin Introduces 'Silence Dogood.'" *Mass Moments*. Massachusetts Foundation for the Humanities, 2015. Web. 25 Feb. 2015. <http://www.massmoments.org/moment.cfm?mid=101>.

"The Birth of Silence Dogood." *Massachusetts Historical Society*. Massachusetts Historical Society, 2015. Web. 11 Feb. 2015. <http://www.masshist.org/online/silence_dogood/essay.php?entry_id=203>.

Franklin, Benjamin. *The Autobiography of Benjamin Franklin (Dover Thrift Editions)*. **New York:** Dover Publications, 1996.

Isaacson, Walter. *Benjamin Franklin: An American Life*. New York: Simon & Schuster, 2004.

"A Quick Biography of Benjamin Franklin." *UShistory.org*. Independence Hall Association, 2014. Web. 11 Feb. 2015. <http://www.ushistory.org/franklin/info/index.htm>.

"What You Can Learn From Benjamin Franklin's Daily Schedule." *Lifehack*. Lifehack.org, 2015. Web. 11 Feb. 2015. <http://www.lifehack.org/articles/productivity/what-you-can-learn-from-benjamin-franklins-daily-schedule.html>.

Mary Ann Evans

Adams, Nene. "Top 10 Truly Weird Victorian Fads." *Listverse*. 7 Nov. 2012. Web. 25 Feb. 2015. <http://listverse.com/2012/11/07/top-10-truly-weird-victorian-fads/>.

Alpin, Maeve. "Did Ya Know Bram Stoker, Poe, & Louisa May Allcott Wrote Mummy tales?" *Steampunk Empire*. Steampunk Empire, 2015. 3 Jul. 2013. Web. 25 Feb. 2015. <http://www.thesteampunkempire.com/forum/topics/did-ya-know-bram-stoker-poe-louisa-may-allcott-wrote-mummy-tales>

"George Eliot (1819-1880)." *BBC*. BBC, 2014. Web. 11 Feb. 2015. <http://www.bbc.co.uk/history/historic_figures/eliot_george.shtml>.

"George Eliot." *Daniel Deronda*. PBS, 2015. Web. 11 Feb. 2015. <http://www.pbs.org/wgbh/masterpiece/deronda/ei_eliot.html>.

"George Eliot / Marian Evans (1819–1880)." *British Humanist Association*. British Humanist Association, 2015. Web. 11 Feb. 2015. <https://humanism.org.uk/humanism/the-humanist-tradition/19th-century-freethinkers/george-eliot/>.

Kirkova, Deni. "Inside the incredible world of Victorian taxidermy: Stuffed kittens dressed in wedding gowns and cigar-smoking squirrels photographed for new book." *Daily Mail*. 21 Apr. 2014. Associated Newspapers Ltd., 2015. Web. 25 Feb. 2015. <http://www.dailymail.co.uk/femail/article-2607024/Inside-incredible-world-Victorian-taxidermy-Stuffed-kittens-dressed-wedding-gowns-cigar-smoking-squirrels-photographed-new-book.html>.

Section 3: Cheaters and Thieves

Chapter 9: Slick Salesmen

Charles Ponzi

"Charles Ponzi." *Bio*. A&E Television Networks, 2015. Web. 11 Feb. 2015. <http://www.biography.com/people/charles-ponzi-20650909>.

Darby, Mary. "In Ponzi We Trust." *Smithsonian Magazine*. Dec. 1998. Smithsonian, 2015. Web. 25 Feb. 2015. <http://www.smithsonianmag.com/people-places/in-ponzi-we-trust-64016168/>.

Knufken, Drea. "The 10 Nastiest Ponzi Schemes Ever." *Business Pundit*. 15 Dec. 2008. Alpha Web Holdings. 25 Feb. 2015. <http://www.businesspundit.com/the-10-nastiest-ponzi-schemes-ever/>.

Ponzi, Charles. *The Rise of Mr. Ponzi: The Autobiography of a Financial Genius*. Digital Mammouth Editions. Web. 11 Feb. 2015. <http://pnzi.com/>.

Zuckoff, Mitchell. *Ponzi's Scheme: The True Story of a Financial Legend*. New York: Random House, 2005.

Victor Lustig

Johnson, James Francis, and Floyd Miller. *The Man Who Sold the Eiffel Tower*. Garden City, NY: Doubleday, 1961.

King, Gilbert. "The Smoothest Con Man That Ever Lived." *Smithsonian.com*. 22 Aug. 2012. Smithsonian, 2015. Web. 25 Feb. 2015. <http://www.smithsonian-mag.com/history/the-smoothest-con-man-that-ever-lived-29861908/>.

"King Con." *Useless Information*. Web. 11 Feb. 2015. <http://uselessinformation.org/lustig/index.html>.

"The major events." *La Tour Eiffel*. SETE, 2010. Web. 11 Feb. 2015. <http://www.toureiffel.paris/en/every-thing-about-the-tower/the-major-events.html>.

Palermo, Elizabeth. "Eiffel Tower: Information & Facts." *Live Science*. 7 May 2013. Purch, 2015. Web. 25 Feb. 2015. <http://www.livescience.com/29391-eiffel-tower.html>.

"Victor Lustig." *Bio*. A&E Television Networks, 2015. Web. 11 Feb. 2015. <http://www.biography.com/people/victor-lustig-20657385#crimes>.

Willett, Megan. "13 Things You Never Knew About The Eiffel Tower." *Business Insider*. 31 Mar. 2014. Business Insider Inc., 2015. Web. 25 Feb. 2015. <http://www.businessinsider.com/eiffel-tower-125th-birthday-facts-2014-3>.

Bernard "Bernie" Madoff

Clark, Josh, and Jane McGrath. "How Ponzi Schemes Work." *HowStuffWorks.com*. 9 Feb. 2009. Web. 25 Feb. 2015. <http://money.howstuffworks.com/ponzi-scheme.htm>.

Glovin, David, and David Scheer. "Madoff Charged in $50 Billion Fraud at Advisory Firm (Update3)." *Bloomberg*. 11 Dec. 2008. Bloomberg, 2015. Web. 25 Feb. 2015. <http://www.bloomberg.com/apps/news?pid=newsarchive&sid=anWXzISP4XCg>.

Italiano, Laura. "Bernie Madoff suffers heart attack in prison." *New York Post*. 22 Jan. 2014. NYP Holdings, 2015. 25 Feb. 2015. <http://nypost.com/2014/01/22/bernie-madoff-suffers-heart-attack-in-prison/>.

Lenzner, Robert. "Bernie Madoff's $50 Billion Ponzi Scheme." *Forbes*. 12 Dec. 2008. Forbes.com, 2015. Web. 25 Feb. 2015. <http://www.forbes.com/2008/12/12/madoff-ponzi-hedge-pf-ii-in_rl_1212croesus_inl.html>.

"The Madoff files: Bernie's billions." *The Independent*. 29 Jan. 2009. Independent.co.uk., 2015. Web. 25 Feb. 2015. <http://www.independent.co.uk/news/business/analysis-and-features/the-madoff-files-bernies-billions-1518939.html>.

"Madoff's Victims." *The Wall Street Journal*. 6 Mar. 2009. WSJ.com, 2015. Web. 25 Feb. 2015. <https://s.wsj.net/public/resources/documents/st_madoff_victims_20081215.html>.

Seal, Mark. "Madoff's World." *Vanity Fair*. Apr. 2009. Conde Nast. Web. 25 Feb. 2015. <http://www.vanityfair.com/politics/features/2009/04/bernard-madoff-friends-family-profile>.

Zambito, Thomas, Jose Martinez, and Corky Siemasz-ko. "By, Bye Bernie: Ponzi king Madoff sentenced to 150 years." *Daily News*. 29 Jun. 2009. NYDailyNews.com, 2015. Web. 25 Feb. 2015. <http://www.nydailynews.com/news/money/bye-bye-bernie-ponzi-king-madoff-sentenced-150-years-article-1.373445>.

Chapter 10: Religious Scammers

Pope Leo X

Doak, Robin S. *Pope Leo X: Opponent of the Reformation*. Mankato, MN: Compass Point Books, 2006.

Duggan, Lawrence G. "Indulgence." *Encyclopædia Britannica*. Encyclopædia Britannica Online. Encyclopædia Britannica Inc., 2015. Web. 9 Feb. 2015. <http://www.britannica.com/EBchecked/topic/286800/indulgence>.

Fitzpatrick, Laura. "Top 10 Controversial Popes: Sergius III." *Time*. 14 Apr. 2010. Time Inc., 2015. Web. 25 Feb. 2015. <http://content.time.com/time/specials/packages/article/0,28804,1981842_1981844_1981869,00.html>.

Gallaher, John G. "Leo X." *Encyclopædia Britannica*. Encyclopædia Britannica Online. Encyclopædia Britannica Inc., 2015. Web. 9 Feb. 2015. britannica.com/EBchecked/topic/336261/Leo-X.>

Graves, Dan. "Infamous Indulgence Led to Reformation." *Christianity.com*. May 2007. Christianity.com, 2015. Web. 11 Feb. 2015. <http://www.christianity.com/church/church-history/timeline/1501-1600/infamous-indulgence-led-to-reformation-11629920.html>.

Howard, Michael. "7 Popes Who Wouldn't Qualify for #TIMEPOY." *Esquire*. 11 Dec. 2013. Hearst Men's Group, 2015. Web. 23 Feb. 2015 <http://www.esquire.com/news-politics/news/a26460/worst-popes-list-1213/>

"Pope Leo X." *Martin Luther*. Devillier Donegan Enterprises, 2003. Web. 11 Feb. 2015. <http://www.pbs.org/empires/martinluther/char_leo.html>.

Sun Myung Moon

Blake, Mariah. "The Fall of the House of Moon." *New Republic*. 12 Nov. 2013. The New Republic, 2015. Web. 25 Feb. 2015. <http://www.newrepublic.com/article/115512/unification-church-profile-fall-house-moon>.

Eng, Monica, Delroy Alexander, and David Jackson. "Sushi and Rev. Moon." *Chicago Tribune*. 11 Apr. 2006. Chicago Tribune, 2015. Web. 25 Feb. 2015. <http://www.chicagotribune.com/news/watchdog/chi-0604sushi-1-story-story.html#page=1>.

Gorenfeld, John. *Bad Moon Rising: How the Reverend Sun Myung Moon Created the Washington Times, Seduced the Religious Right, and Built His Kingdom*. Sausalito, CA: PoliPointPress, 2008..

Parry, Robert. "How Rev. Moon's 'Snakes' Infested US." *Consortiumnews.com.* 2 Sep. 2012. Consortiumnews, 2013. Web. 25 Feb. 2015. <https://consortiumnews.com/2012/09/02/how-rev-moons-snakes-infested-us/>.

Wakin, Daniel J. "Rev. Sun Myung Moon, Self-Proclaimed Messiah Who Built Religious Movement, Dies at 92." *The New York Times.* 2 Sept. 2012. The New York Times Co., 2015. Web. 25 Feb. 2015. <http://www.nytimes.com/2012/09/03/world/asia/rev-sun-myung-moon-founder-of-unification-church-dies-at-92.html?pagewanted=all&_r=1&>

Wetzstein, Cheryl. "Rev. Moon, Times founder, dies at 92." *The Washington Times.* 2 Sep. 2012. The Washington Times, 2015. Web. 25 Feb. 2015. <http://www.washingtontimes.com/news/2012/sep/2/rev-sun-myung-moon-founder-times-dies-92/?page=all>.

Peter Popoff

Blair, Leonardo. "Controversial Televangelist Peter Popoff Hawks 'Miracle Water.'" *The Christian Post.* 4 Apr. 2013. The Christian Post, 2015. Web. 25 Feb. 2015. <http://www.christianpost.com/news/controversial-televangelist-peter-popoff-hawks-miracle-water-93290/>.

Eric. "6 Outrageously Wealthy Preachers Under Federal Investigation." *Avvo Naked Law.* 4 Jun. 2010. Avvo, Inc., 2015. Web. 25 Feb. 2015. <http://nakedlaw.avvo.com/money/6-outrageously-wealthy-preachers-under-federal-investigation.html>.

Golgowski, Nina. "Private jets, 13 mansions and a $100,000 mobile home just for the dogs: Televangelists defrauded tens of million of dollars from Christian network.'" *Daily Mail.* 23 Mar. 2012. Associated Newspapers. Web. 25 Feb. 2015. <http://www.dailymail.co.uk/news/article-2119493/Private-jets-13-mansions-100-000-mobile-home-just-dogs-Televangelists-defrauded-tens-million-dollars-Christian-network.html>.

"The Hall of Shame." *Famous TV Evangelists.* 18 Apr. 2011. Web. 11 Feb. 2015. <http://theevangelists.blogspot.com/2011/04/hall-of-shame.html>.

Harrison, Kristi. "The 5 Ballsiest Con Artists of All Time." *Cracked.* 13 Feb. 2008. Demand Media, 2013. <http://www.cracked.com/article_15892_the-5-ballsiest-con-artists-all-time.html>.

Higginbotham, Adam. "The Unbelievable Skepticism of the Amazing Randi." *The New York Times Magazine.* 7 Nov. 2014. The New York Times Co., 2015. Web. 23 Feb. 2015. <http://www.nytimes.com/2014/11/09/magazine/the-unbelievable-skepticism-of-the-amazing-randi.html?_r=0>.

Maag, Christopher. "Scam Everlasting: After 25 Years, Debunked Faith Healer Still Preaching Debt Relief Scam." *Business Insider.* 22 Sep. 2011. Business Insider Inc., 2015. Web. 25 Feb. 2015. <http://www.businessinsider.com/scam-everlasting-after-25-years-debunked-faith-healer-still-preaching-debt-relief-scam-2011-9>.

MacArthur, John. "Measuring Oral Roberts's Influence." *Grace to You.* 2015. Web. 11 Feb. 2015. <https://www.gty.org/Resources/Print/Blog/B091218>.

Randi, James. *The Faith Healers.* Buffalo, NY: Prometheus Books, 1989.

Seckel, Al. "God's Frequency is 39.17 MHz: The Investigation of Peter Popoff." *Science and the Paranormal.* 1987. Web. 11 Feb. 2015. <http://casa.colorado.edu/~dduncan/pseudoscience/PeterPopoff.htm>.

Smith, Kenneth L. "The Televangelists' Hall of Shame." 1998. Web. 11 Feb. 2015. <http://home.earthlink.net/~19ranger57/halosham.htm>.

"Oral Roberts." *The Telegraph.* 16 Dec. 2009. Telegraph Media Group, 2015. Web. 25 Feb. 2015. <http://www.telegraph.co.uk/news/obituaries/religion-obituaries/6827907/Oral-Roberts.html>.

"Pat Robertson's Age-Defying Shake." *CBN.com.* The Christian Broadcasting Network, Inc., 2015. Web. 11 Feb. 2015. <http://www.cbn.com/communitypublic/shake.aspx>.

Thorpe, G. "8 Black Pastors Whose Net Worth is 200 Times Greater Than Folks in Their Local Communities." *Atlanta Black Star.* 26 Jun. 2014. AtlantaBlackStar.com, 2015. Web. 25 Feb. 2015. <http://atlantablackstar.com/2014/06/26/8-black-pastors-whose-net-worth-is-200-times-greater-than-folks-in-their-local-community/2/>.

Zoll, Rachel. "Televangelists escape penalty in Senate inquiry." *Associated Press.* 7 Jan. 2011. Associated Press, 2011. Web. 25 Feb. 2015. <http://www.nbcnews.com/id/40960871/ns/politics-capitol_hill/t/televangelists-escape-penalty-senate-inquiry/#.VLfbZ8t0yUm>.

Chapter 11: Cheaters Never Win (Except When They Do)

Charles Van Doren

"About Ken." *Ken Jennings.* 2015. Web. 11 Feb. 2015. <http://www.ken-jennings.com/about>.

"Charles Van Doren." *The Quiz Show Scandal.* PBS Online, WGBH, 1999. Web. 11 Feb. 2015. <http://www.pbs.org/wgbh/amex/quizshow/peopleevents/pande02.html>.

MacDonald, J. Fred. "The Quiz Show Scandals." *One Nation Under Television: the Rise and Decline of Network TV.* 2009. Web. 12 Feb. 2015. <http://jfredmacdonald.com/onutv/quiz.htm>.

"Quiz Show." *Internet Movie Database*. IMDb.com, Inc., 2015. Web. 11 Feb. 2015. <http://www.imdb. com/title/tt0110932/>.

Van Doren, Charles. "All the Answers." *The New Yorker*. 28 Jul. 2008. Conde Nast. Web. 11 Feb. 2015. <http://www.newyorker.com/magazine/2008/07/28/ all-the-answers>.

Rosie Ruiz

Amdur, Neil. "Who Is Rosie Ruiz?" *The New York Times*. 21 Apr. 1980. The New York Times Company, 2004. Web. 25 Feb. 2015. <http://www.nytimes.com/ packages/html/sports/year_in_sports/04.21.html>.

"Boston Marathon History: Boston Marathon Facts." The Boston Marathon. Web. 25 Feb. 2015. <http:// www.baa.org/races/boston-marathon/boston-mara-thon-history/boston-marathon-facts.aspx>.

Fox, Kit. "Oldest Youngest Entrants Finish Boston Marathon." *Newswire*. 22 Apr. 2014. Runner's World, 2015. Web. 25 Feb. 2015. <http://www.runnersworld. com/boston-marathon/oldest-youngest-entrants-finish-boston-marathon>.

"History of the Marathon." *Marathon Greece*. Web. 11 Feb. 2015. <http://www.marathongreece.com/ marathonhistory.html>.

Maloney, Paula. "Where are they now: Rosie Ruiz and the man who uncovered her ruse." *She's Game Sports*. 30 Mar. 2013. Boston.com. Web. 25 Feb. 2015. <http://www.boston.com/sports/blogs/shesgames-ports/2013/03/where-are-they-now-rosie-ruiz-and-the-man-who-uncovered-her-ruse.html>.

Roberts, Sam. "The Moxie of Rosie Ruiz, New York Marathon Runner." *Huffington Post*. 31 Oct. 2014. TheHuffingtonPost.com, Inc., 2015. Web. 25 Feb. 2015. <http://www.huffingtonpost.com/sam-roberts/ the-moxie-of-rosie-ruiz-n_b_6084132.html>.

"Rosie Ruiz Wins the Boston Marathon." *The New York Times*. 30 Apr. 1980. Web. 25 Feb. 2015. <http:// hoaxes.org/archive/permalink/rosie_ruiz_wins_the_ boston_marathon>.

Sebor, Jessica. "26.2 facts about the Boston Marathon." *WomensRunning.com*. 30 Jul. 2013. ESPN.com, 2015. Web. 25 Feb. 2015. <http://espn.go.com/blog/endur-ance/post/_/id/1527/26-2-facts-about-the-boston-marathon>.

Lance Armstrong

"Chairman Bill's History of the Tour de France: Origins and Early Years." *BikeRaceInfo*. McGann Publishing. Web. 16 Feb. 2015. <http://www.bikeraceinfo.com/ tdf/tdf%20history/tdfhistory1900.html>.

"Lance Armstrong Bio." *Support for Lance*. 2015. Web. 16 Feb. 2015. <http://www.lancesupport.org/bio. php>.

"Lance Armstrong Biography." *Kidzworld*. Kidzworld, 2015. Web. 16 Feb. 2015. <http://www.kidzworld. com/article/3667-lance-armstrong-biography>.

Linden, Julian. "Armstrong admits doping in 'toxic' tale." *Reuters*. 18 Jan. 2013. Thomson Reuters, 2015. Web. 25 Feb. 2015. <http://www.reuters.com/ article/2013/01/18/us-cycling-armstrong-admitting-idUSBRE90H04620130118>.

Majendie, Matt. "Lance Armstrong: 'Day-to-day life is positive.'" *CNN*. 20 Aug. 2014. Cable News Network, 2015. Web. 25 Feb. 2015. <http://edition. cnn.com/2014/08/19/sport/lance-armstrong-doping-cycling/>.

OWN TV. "Lance Armstrong's Confession: Oprah's Next Chapter: Oprah Winfrey Network." Online video. *YouTube*. 17 Jan. 2013. Web. 25 Feb. 2015. <https://www.youtube.com/ watch?v=N_0PSZ59Aws>.

Richardson, John H. "Lance Armstrong in Purga-tory: The After-Life." *Esquire*. 7 Jul. 2014. Hearst Communications, Inc., 2015. Web. 25 Feb. 2015. <http://www.esquire.com/features/lance-armstrong-interview-0814>.

Schrotenboer, Brent. "Lance Armstrong Must Pay $10 Million in Perjury Battle." *USA Today*. 16 Feb. 2015. Gannett Satellite Information Network, Inc., 2015. Web. 23 Feb. 2015. < http://www.usatoday.com/ story/sports/cycling/tourdefrance/2015/02/16/lance-armstrong-sca-promotions-ruling/23496931/>

Section 4: Aliens, Ghosts, and Creature Hoaxes

Chapter 12: Little Space People

Don Weiss, LeRoy Schultz, and Jerry Sprague

"Alien abduction." *The Skeptic's Dictionary*. 12 Sep. 2014. Robert T. Carroll, 2015. Web. 25 Feb. 2015. <http://skepdic.com/aliens.html>.

Clancy, Susan A. *Abducted: How People Come to Believe They Were Kidnapped by Aliens*. Cambridge, MA: Harvard University Press, 2005.

Jenkins, Beverly. "10 Amazing Alien Abduction Stories." *Oddee*. 28 Sep. 2011. Oddee, 2015. Web. 25 Feb. 2015. <http://www.oddee.com/item_97917. aspx>.

"The Little Blue Man Hoax." *The Museum of Hoaxes*. Alex Boese, 2014. Web. 16 Feb. 2015. <http://hoaxes. org/archive/permalink/the_little_blue_man_hoax>.

Shermer, Michael. *Why People Believe Weird Things: Pseudoscience, Superstition, and Other Confusions of Our Time*. New York: W.H. Freeman, 1997.

Sagan, Carl, and Ann Druyan. *The Demon-Haunted World: Science as a Candle in the Dark*. New York: Random House, 1996. Weisenbach, Traci L. "50 years ago, 'Little Blue Man' shook up Elkton." *Huron Daily Tribune*. 31 Oct. 2008. Huron Daily Tribune, 2015. Web. 25 Feb. 2015. <http://www.michigansthumb. com/news/local/article_69c6254d-1229-5d48-956f-760a2833719a.html>.

Doug Bower and Dave Chorley

Eddie, Laurie. "The Skeptics SA Guide to: Crop circles." *Skeptics SA*. 4 Nov. 2004. Web. 25 Feb. 2015. <http://www.skepticssa.org.au/html/cropcircles.html>.

"The Human Butterfly: Biggest Crop Circle Ever!" *Psychedelic Adventure*. Aug. 2009. Psychedelic Adventure, 2014. Web. 25 Feb. 2015. <http://www.psychedelicadventure.net/2009/09/human-butterfly-biggest-crop-circle.html>.

Mayell, Hillary. "Crop Circles: Artworks of Alien Signs?" *National Geographic News*. 2 Aug. 2002. National Geographic Society, 2015. Web. 25 Feb. 2015. <http://news.nationalgeographic.com/news/2002/08/0801_020801_cropcircles.html>.

Nickell, Joe. "Circular Reasoning: The 'Mystery' of Crop Circles and Their 'Orbs' of Light." *Skeptical Inquirer*. Vol. 26.5. Sep./Oct. 2002. Web. 25 Feb. 2015. <http://www.csicop.org/si/show/circular_reasoning_the_mystery_of_crop_circles_and_their_orbs_of_light/>.

Schmidt, William E. "2 'Jovial Con Men' Demystify Those Crop Circles in Britain." *The New York Times*. 10 Sep. 1991. The New York Times Company, 2015. 25 Feb. 2015. <http://www.nytimes.com/1991/09/10/world/2-jovial-con-men-demystify-those-crop-circles-in-britain.html>.

Southworth, June. "Confessions of the Crop Circle Conman." *Daily Mail*. 8 Jan. 1999. Daily Mail, 2007. Web 25 Feb. 2015. <http://www.highbeam.com/doc/1G1-109776483.html>.

Ray Santilli

"Alien Autopsy." *The Museum of Hoaxes*. Alex Boese, 2014. Web. 16 Feb. 2015. <http://hoaxes.org/archive/permalink/alien_autopsy>.

Eamonn Investigates: Alien Autopsy. Presented by Eamonn Holmes. Sky, 2006.

International UFO Museum Research Center. IUFOM-RC NM Inc., 2010. Web. 25 Feb. 2015. <http://www.roswellufomuseum.com/>.

"New Twist In Decades Old Alien Autopsy Controversy (Graphic Video)." *The Huffington Post*. 11 Dec. 2013. TheHuffingtonPost.com, Inc., 2015. Web 25 Feb. 2015. <http://www.huffingtonpost.com/2013/12/10/russia-alien-autopsy-crashed-ufo_n_4411271.html>.

Nickell, Joe. "The Story Behind the 'Alien Autopsy' Hoax." *Live Science*. 7 May 2006. Purch, 2015. Web. 25 Feb. 2015. <http://www.livescience.com/742-story-alien-autopsy-hoax.html>.

"Ray Santilli." *Internet Movie Database*. IMDb.com, Inc., 2015. Web. 25 Feb. 2015. <http://www.imdb.com/name/nm1904513/>.

Chapter 13: Scary Creatures

George Hull

"Cardiff." *TripAdvisor*. TripAdvisor, 2015. Web. 16 Feb. 2015. <http://www.tripadvisor.com/Tourism-g186460-Cardiff_Southern_Wales_Wales-Vacations.html>.

"The Cardiff Giant." *The Farmers' Museum*. The New York State Historical Association. Web. 16 Feb. 2015. <http://www.farmersmuseum.org/node/2482>.

"The Cardiff Giant." *The Museum of Hoaxes*. Alex Boese, 2014. Web. 16 Feb. 2015. <http://hoaxes.org/archive/permalink/the_cardiff_giant>.

"Cardiff Giant." *The Skeptic's Dictionary*. 15 Dec. 2013. Robert T. Carroll, 2015. Web. 25 Feb. 2015. <http://skepdic.com/cardiff.html>.

"The FAMILY ghost walk." *Cardiff History and Hauntings*. 2015. Web. 16 Feb. 2015. <http://www.cardiffhistory.co.uk/index.php?p=28>.

"The Great Cardiff Giant." Donald Simanek. Web. 16 Feb. 2015. <https://www.lhup.edu/~dsimanek/cardiff.htm>.

Lambert, Tim. "A Brief History Of Cardiff, Wales." *A World History Encyclopedia*. Web. 16 Feb. 2015. <http://www.localhistories.org/Cardiff.html>.

Marmaduke Wetherall

Coville, C. "5 Myths That People Don't Realize Are Admitted Hoaxes." *Cracked*. 18 Oct. 2009. Demand Media, 2013. Web. 25 Feb. 2015. <http://www.cracked.com/article/157_5-myths-that-people-dont-realize-are-admitted-hoaxes/>.

Josephson, Joan. "History, Great Dane defy rain at Brocton-Portland festival." *Observer Today*. 12 Jul. 2009. Observer Today, 2015. Web. 25 Feb. 2015. <http://www.observertoday.com/page/content.detail/id/526356.html?nav=5047>.

Krystek, Lee. "Nessie of Loch Ness." *The Museum of UnNatural Mystery*. 2007. Web. 16 Feb. 2015. <http://www.unmuseum.org/lochness.htm>.

"Loch Ness Monster, 'Nessie.'" *Monsters of the Sea*. Rutgers, 2008. Web. 16 Feb. 2015. <http://rucool.marine.rutgers.edu/monsters/monsters_loch_ness1.html>.

Lyons, Stephen. "The Legend of Loch Ness." *NOVA*. 12 Jan. 1999. PBS Online, WGBH, 2015. Web. 25 Feb. 2015. <http://www.pbs.org/wgbh/nova/ancient/legend-loch-ness.html>.

Summers, Nick. "Google Maps' new transport options: A dragon, the Loch Ness Monster and a royal carriage." *The Next Web*. 4 Jun. 2014. The Next Web, 2015. Web. 25 Feb. 2015. <http://thenextweb.com/google/2014/06/04/google-maps-easter-eggs/>.

"The Surgeon's Photo." *The Museum of Hoaxes*. Alex Boese, 2014. Web. 16 Feb. 2015. <http://hoaxes.org/photo_database/image/the_surgeons_photo/>.

Big Foot Hunters

The Bigfoot Field Researchers Organization. BFRO.net, 2015. Web. 16 Feb. 2015. <http://www.bfro.net/>.

"Bigfoot Hoaxes." *The Museum of Hoaxes.* Alex Boese, 2014. Web. 16 Feb. 2014. <http://hoaxes.org/archive/display/category/bigfoot>.

Bush, Ed, and Terry Gaston. "Wildman of the Woods: An Encounter with Bigfoot." *Inexact Science.* 1977. Web. 16 Feb. 2015. <https://oddbooks.co.uk/odd-books/wildman-woods>.

"The Cherie Darvell 'Kidnapped by Bigfoot' 1976 Story." *The Record-Searchlight Newspaper.* 8 Feb. 1978. Bigfoot Encounters, 2011. Web. 16 Feb. 2015. <http://www.bigfootencounters.com/articles/humboldt.htm>.

Korff, Kal K., and Michaela Kocis. "Exposing Roger Patterson's 1967 Bigfoot Film Hoax." *Skeptical Inquirer.* Jul./Aug. 2004. Bigfoot Encounters, 2011. Web. 16 Feb. 2015. <http://www.bigfootencounters.com/articles/korff04.htm>.

"Occam's razor." *Encyclopædia Britannica. Encyclopædia Britannica Online.* Encyclopædia Britannica Inc., 2015. Web. 9 Feb. 2015. <http://www.britannica.com/EBchecked/topic/424706/Occams-razor>.

Radford, Benjamin. "New 'Bigfoot' Sighting Latest in Series of Hoaxes." *Discovery News.* 3 Oct. 2013. Discovery Communications, 2015. Web. 25 Feb. 2015. <http://news.discovery.com/animals/new-bigfoot-sighting-just-latest-in-series-of-hoaxes-131003.htm>.

Radford, Benjamin. "Bigfoot: Man-Monster or Myth?" *Live Science.* 6 Nov. 2012. Purch, 2015. Web. 25 Feb. 2015. <http://www.livescience.com/24598-bigfoot.html>.

Sanderson, Ivan T. "The Strange Story of AMERICA'S ABOMINABLE SNOWMAN." *True Magazine.* Dec. 1959. Bigfoot Encounters, 2011. Web. 16 Feb. 2015. <http://www.bigfootencounters.com/articles/true1959.htm>.

Chapter 14: Boo! Ghosts and Spirits

Frances Griffiths and Elsie Wright

Briggs, Katharine. *An Encyclopedia of Fairies, Hobgoblins, Brownies, Bogies, and Other Supernatural Creatures.* [1976]. Middlesex, United Kingdom: Penguin, 1977.

"The case of the Cottingley fairies." Donald Simanek, 2013. Web. 16 Feb. 2015. <http://www.lhup.edu/~dsimanek/cooper.htm>.

Castelow, Ellen. "The Origins of Fairies." *Historic UK.* Historic UK, 2015. Web. 16 Feb. 2015. <http://www.historic-uk.com/CultureUK/The-Origins-of-Fairies/>.

"The Cottingley Fairies." *The Museum of Hoaxes.* Alex Boese, 2014. Web. 16 Feb. 2015. <http://hoaxes.org/photo_database/image/the_cottingley_fairies/>.

Krystek, Lee. "The Case of the Cottingley Fairies." *The Museum of UnNatural Mystery.* 2000. Web. 16 Feb. 2015. <http://www.unmuseum.org/fairies.htm>.

"A Mermaid and a Magic Comb." *Myths and Legends.* E2BN, 2006. Web. 16 Feb. 2015. <http://myths.e2bn.org/mythsandlegends/origins532-a-mermaid-and-a-magic-comb.html>.

Monaghan, Patricia. *Encyclopedia of Goddesses and Heroines* [2 volumes]. ABC-CLIO, 2009.

Page, Michael, and Robert Ingpen. *British Goblins: Encyclopedia of Things That Never Were.* New York: Viking, 1987.

Anne Moberly and Eleanor Jourdain

Castle, Terry. "Contagious Folly: *An Adventure* and Its Skeptics." *Critical Inquiry.* Vol. 17, No. 45 (Summer, 1991). University of Chicago Press, 1991. 741–72. <http://www.jstor.org/discover/10.2307/1343742?sid=21105240367821&uid=4&uid=2129&uid=70&uid=2&uid=3739256&uid=3739928>.

"The Ghosts of Versailles." *The Museum of Hoaxes.* Alex Boese, 2014. Web. 16 Feb. 2015. <http://hoaxes.org/versailles.html>.

Richardson, Tim. "Are there really ghosts at Versailles?" *The Telegraph.* 21 Dec. 2012. Telegraph Media Group, 2015. Web. 25 Feb. 2015. <http://www.telegraph.co.uk/gardening/gardenstovisit/9756398/Are-there-really-ghosts-at-Versailles.html>.

"Shared Psychotic Disorder Symptoms." *Psych Central.* Psych Central, 2015. Web. 16 Feb. 2015. <http://psychcentral.com/disorders/shared-psychotic-disorder-symptoms/>.

"Versailles in Florida: Construction Resumes on Biggest House in US." *ABC News.* 1 Oct. 2013. ABC News Internet Ventures, 2015. Web. 25 Feb. 2015. <http://abcnews.go.com/blogs/lifestyle/2013/10/versailles-in-florida-construction-resumes-on-biggest-house-in-us/>.

Ghostwatch

Angelini, Sergio. "Ghostwatch (1992)." *BFI Screenonline.* BFI Screenonline, 2014. Web. 16 Feb. 2015. <http://www.screenonline.org.uk/tv/id/715896/>.

"Ghostly Facts." *Legends of America.* Legends of America, 2015. Web. 16 Feb. 2015. <http://www.legendsofamerica.com/gh-ghostfacts.html>.

"Ghostwatch." *The Museum of Hoaxes.* Alex Boese, 2014. Web. 16 Feb. 2015. <http://hoaxes.org/ghostwatch.html>.

Lawden, Rich. *Ghostwatch.* Web. 16 Feb. 2015. <http://www.ghostwatchbtc.com/>.

Simons, D., and W.R. Silveira. "Post-traumatic stress disorder in children after television programmes." *British Medical Journal.* V.308(6925). 5 Feb. 1994. PMC. Web. 16 Feb. 2015. <http://www.ncbi.nlm.nih.gov/pmc/articles/PMC2539494/>.

Volk, Stephen. "Ghostwatch." *Stephenvolk.net.* Web. 16 Feb. 2015. <http://www.stephenvolk.net/page19.htm>.

CHRISTINE SEIFERT is a native North Dakotan and a professor at Westminster College in Salt Lake City, Utah. She is the author of the novel *The Predicteds*, as well as the nonfiction book *The Endless Wait: Virginity in Young Adult Literature*. She writes for *Bitch Magazine* and other publications, and has presented at academic conferences on such diverse topics as as writing, rhetoric, *Twilight*, and *Jersey Shore*.